The DocNet

The Free Market Solution to Replace Obamacare
and the Plan to Save America's Healthcare System
from Socialized Medicine & Government Control

By Keven M. Card

Copyright © 2012 Keven M. Card

CreateSpace Edition

Published by Keven Card and Storehouse Publishing,
Humble, TX.

This title may be purchased in bulk for educational,
business, fund-raising, or sales promotional use. For
information please email: info@kevencard.com

Table of Contents

Introduction

We have a problem in America with our healthcare! But it's not a crisis in care, it's the escalating cost of that care, and is hitting us all where it really hurts, our pocketbooks. At the beginning of the Obama Administration, it was decided that the government would solve the, quote, "healthcare crisis".

A "crisis", really?

I mean, we all know that we had (and still have) a severe cost problem, which is developing into a crisis, because our premium continues to skyrocket, and at the same time, the economy is receding which only makes it worse. But, in spite of the public outcry, and governors pleading with their Senators not to pass healthcare reform, what we call Obamacare was pushed through with arm twisting, behind closed doors deal making and bureaucratic manipulation. Now, just over two years later and in the heat of a Presidential election year, this is just one of the laws being used for the same old Washington games of political posturing and frankly, the American people have grown tired of these games.

Our healthcare is important to us, and we don't want it to be used to gain political points, we want real solutions to solve the cost crisis of our healthcare. I don't believe that most Americans support a new massive overhaul of the healthcare industry by politicians in Washington. What we want are real solutions to this important issue, but the question is, and what we need to decide, is who has the better option, the government or the free market?

For the last twenty years, I've spent my professional life, selling health and supplemental insurance, and it's my opinion that the free market is far better equipped to create and manage a real solution to address the cost concerns that we all have. In this book, I will point out some of the flaws of the government's attempt to solve this problem and then I will present to you an authentic, free market solution that can be implemented without raising taxes, growing the size of our government, or creating more dependency on entitlements. Oh, and I should mention that it comes with NO government investment required.

Now, I will say that I don't have a crystal ball and I am certainly not the only person out there that may have an alternative solution to Obamacare. But, it is my hope that this book will start a real conversation about how to solve this very important problem, while avoiding the tragedy of socialized medicine, or some other government control of our healthcare and insurance industries.

What I'm 100% certain of, is that the American free market has the answers that will solve this very delicate problem, without Constitutional, legislative or financial concerns like we have with Obamacare. If Washington and the state bureaucrats would get out of the way of the free market and the American Entrepreneur they'd find so many solutions, they would question the reason for their existence. As Ronald Reagan famously said: "Government is not the solution to the problem, government is the problem", and what was true then is true now. Anyway, enough bashing let's get onto to the solutions.

Chapter 1

The Constitutionality of Obamacare

The Supreme Court heard arguments for three days in March of 2012 and is expected to render its opinion in June on whether or not the Healthcare Reform Act commonly referred to as "Obamacare" is constitutional. Twenty-seven states have filed lawsuits against the federal government alleging that the law supersedes their authority by creating an individual mandate to purchase health insurance. This was done by a government controlled by Democrats, with no Republican support, and in the face of an America uprising in opposition to the notion of government controlled healthcare. Now, the Supreme Court will be the one to determine if the commerce clause grants the federal government, any authority to force individuals, as a condition of citizenship, to purchase health insurance.

The decision, which is expected in June of 2012, will have enormous and long lasting ramifications, no matter the outcome of that decision. It will set the tone of either an unlimited ability for the federal government to gain and hold power or grant the states authority to push back against the tide of an overreaching Washington.

The fact is that at no point in the history of this country, has such an attempt been made to control such a vast amount of the American economy; nor has a mandate for the purchase of a product or service ever been tried, and dare I say, every even thought of, at least by those who respect the Constitution. And so, we embark into uncharted waters when it comes to powers that have been granted our government and what freedoms and responsibilities belong to us. What we should all agree on, is that it is, or at least it should be, the responsibility of the individual to take measures to minimize their personal risks and to fund the risks they take; without ever imposing those risks or their costs, on responsible Americans.

However, that doesn't seem to be the case any longer; so, what responsible Americans are asking is: does the irresponsibility of some, give enough cause for the government to take control of the entire healthcare and insurance industries, through mandates and entitlement programs? And to make those same Americans pay the additional expense of the irresponsible, through higher taxes, fees and penalties? Where's the 'fairness' in that?

Back In Time

This isn't the first time America has faced these and similar questions, and it is through history that we find the answer.

If anyone knew the need for healthcare at the beginning of our Republic, it was Ben Franklin. During the writing of the Constitution, Franklin was unable to walk as a result of kidney stones and had to be carried by prisoners to and from Pennsylvania State House where they were drafting our Founding Documents. Even though he suffered immense pain, he never suggested national healthcare in any form. If healthcare is a right of the people and if it's the responsibility of the government to care for its citizen's, as it often suggested today; why was it never made an issue at the creation of America? Common sense would suggest that the health of the population would've been a major issue to the people during the founding era. The argument certainly could've been made that the general welfare clause gave them ample justification to create a national healthcare program or hospital chain, but it simply never was. Why?

That didn't mean Franklin didn't want to resolve the issue at the time, he just knew that the politicians in Washington wouldn't provide the right answer. So, instead when his friend Dr. Bond presented an idea for a public hospital, he went to the citizens and the local assembly to gain support and raise the funds for the creation of the nation's first hospital:

Dr. Bond and Franklin's hospital, Pennsylvania Hospital, still exists today, and this is the story of its founding according to the hospital's website:

Pennsylvania Hospital was founded in 1751 by Dr. Thomas Bond and Benjamin Franklin "to care for the sick-poor and insane who were wandering the streets of Philadelphia." At the time, Philadelphia was the fastest growing city in the 13 colonies. In 1730, the population numbered 11,500 and had grown to 15,000 by 1750 (the city continued to grow and by

1776, its 40,000 residents made Philadelphia the second largest English-speaking city in the British Empire).

The docks and wharves along the Delaware River teemed with activity as ships bound for foreign ports loaded up with flour, meat and lumber while overseas vessels delivered European-manufactured goods and wines. Foreign visitors noted with envy the city's growing prosperity. Although the majority of the population was neither extremely wealthy nor extremely poor, there was a significant increase in the number of immigrant settlers who were "aged, impotent or diseased."

At the time, colonial America's urban centers were far healthier than their European counterparts. Nevertheless, the Philadelphia region, according to city leaders of the day, was "a melting pot for diseases, where Europeans, Africans and Indians engaged in free exchange of their respective infections." Faced with increasing numbers of the poor who were suffering from physical illness and the increasing numbers of people from all classes suffering from mental illness, civic-minded leaders sought a partial solution to the problem by founding a hospital.

The idea for the hospital originated with Dr. Thomas Bond. Born in Calvert County, Maryland, Bond, a Quaker, moved to Philadelphia as a young man. In 1738, in order to further his medical education, he went abroad to study medicine in London. While in Europe, Bond spent time at the famous French hospital, the Hotel-Dieu in Paris, and became impressed with the continent's new hospital movement. Bond returned to Philadelphia in 1739 and two years later was appointed Port Inspector for Contagious Diseases.

Bond and Benjamin Franklin were long-standing friends. Bond was a member of Franklin's Library Company and helped establish the American Philosophical Society and the Academy of Philadelphia, which evolved into the University of Pennsylvania.

Around 1750, Bond "conceived the idea of establishing a hospital in Philadelphia for the reception and cure of poor sick persons." The idea was a novelty on this side of the Atlantic, and when Bond approached Philadelphians for support they asked him what Franklin thought of the idea. Bond hadn't approached his good friend because he thought it was out of Franklin's line of interest, but because of the reaction he received, Bond soon turned to Franklin. After hearing the plan, Franklin became a subscriber and strong supporter. Franklin's backing was enough to convince many others that Bond's projected hospital was worthy of support.

Franklin organized a petition, although not signed by him, bearing 33 names and brought it to the Pennsylvania Assembly on January 20, 1751. The petition stated that although the Pennsylvania Assembly had made many compassionate and charitable provisions for the relief of the poor, a small provincial hospital was necessary. After a second reading on January 28, the petitioners were directed to present the Assembly with a bill to create a hospital. Presented a week later, the bill encouraged the Assembly to establish a hospital "to care for the sick poor of the Province and for the reception and care of lunaticks."

The hospital bill met with some objections from rural members of the Assembly because they thought the hospital would only be serviceable to the city. At this critical juncture, Franklin saved the day with a clever plan to counter the claim by challenging the Assembly that he could prove the populace supported the hospital bill by agreeing to raise 2000 pounds from private citizens. If he was able to raise the funds, Franklin proposed, the Assembly had to match the funds with an additional 2000 pounds. The Assembly agreed to Franklin's plan, thinking his task was impossible, but they were ready to receive the "credit of being charitable without the expense."

Franklin's fundraising effort brought in more than the required amount. The Assembly signed the bill and presented it to Lieutenant Governor James Hamilton for approval. After amending the bill several times, Hamilton signed it into law on May 11, 1751.

From early 1752 until the east wing of the Pine Building opened in 1755 Pennsylvania Hospital was housed in the home of recently deceased John Kinsey, a Quaker and Speaker of the Assembly.

So pleased was Franklin that he later stated: "I do not remember any of my political manoeuvres, the success of which gave me at the time more pleasure..."

To illustrate the purpose of the hospital, the inscription "Take care of him and I will repay thee" was chosen and the image of the Good Samaritan was affixed as the hospital seal.

Even after having had success with the Philadelphia assembly in the creation of a public hospital and knowing the importance of healthcare for the people; it begs the additional question of why there is no evidence to suggest that Franklin ever attempted to gain national support for a centralized hospital program, even though the need for hospitals clearly existed.

If it were the intention of the Founding Fathers to create a system that solved the problems of its citizens; it's obvious that healthcare would've been a matter of much more importance and it's nearly guaranteed that Franklin would've promoted and likely gained adequate support for the endeavor. Especially considering the mass amount of infectious diseases caused just by the social proximity of people from different cultures and the lack of disease control measures available at the time, as was the case in Philadelphia.

Ben Franklin has been quoted as saying: *"When the people find they can vote themselves money that will herald the end of the republic."*

Isn't that exactly what happening, when people continue to vote for politicians who want to create and expand entitlement programs, especially those recipients of social programs who aren't contributing anything by way of paying taxes?

History more than suggests that Franklin knew that the needs of the people were best provided by governments at the local level, and not some national bureaucracy. Because local governments were to closest to the community where the specific needs were know and could be met. Franklin clearly understood that, as a people, we couldn't depend on the national government to provide for the social needs of the people, things like healthcare. That's the reason he sought help from the local assembly of Philadelphia and never once addressed the healthcare issue in debates while framing the Constitution.

Another outspoken historical critic of today's entitlement politicians was James Madison, who was the author of the Bill of Rights and our fourteenth President. How was he outspoken about today's entitlement programs? Because, today's politicians use the general welfare clause of the Constitution to promote entitlement creation and spending. Well, let's just say that he had something to say about the general welfare clause. He explains:

If Congress can employ money indefinitely to the "general welfare," and are the sole and supreme judges of the "general welfare," then they may take the care of religion into their own hands; they may appoint teachers in every state, county, and parish and pay them out of their public treasury; they may take into their own hands the education of children, establishing in like manner schools throughout the United States; they may assume the provision for the poor; they may undertake the regulation of all roads other than post-roads; in short, everything from the highest object of state legislation down to the most minute object of police would be thrown under the power of Congress, for every object I have mentioned would admit of the application of money, and might be called, if Congress pleased, provisions for the "general welfare."

With a few things that the government has yet to accomplish, it sounds very much like the government we have today. I would propose to you that all the governmental structure that has been created since early 1900 is unconstitutional, and would not have ever been considered by those who used the Constitution as the basis for their governance. Yes, the needs of the people should be addressed, but by always putting the freedom of the individual as its highest priority, which can only be done by government at the local level.

Socializing healthcare by means of a federal mandate restricts the individual freedoms of our citizens. Freedom dictates that we have the right to choose which commerce we will participate in. If we're clear about the Constitution's purpose, as a means by which the people restrict the activities of government and not a vehicle by which to provide for its people; then it's clear that Obamacare and other similar laws are a purposeful infringement of our freedoms and must be called out as to what they are, unconstitutional.

To force any individual, as a condition of citizenship, to purchase a product of any kind goes against every non-revisionist truth we know about our country's founding. The powers originally granted to the federal government were the right to "referee" commerce between states and for the common defense ... and, of course, to deliver the mail six days a week.

Chapter 2

The Road to Obamacare

It is my contention that we've arrived at this point as a direct result of the passage of the 17th Amendment, 1 where Senatorial elections were changed from state legislatures to a popular vote of the people, thereby eliminating the voice of the states in the balance of powers.

Now we have both houses of Congress answering to the people instead of one branch answering to the elected officials of the state, which was evident during the debates that led to the passage of Obamacare. Governors were contacting their Senators and pleading with them to vote against healthcare reform.

For example: In a strongly worded letter to Senators Mark Warner and Jim Webb the Lt. Governor of Virginia William Bolling wrote:

DECEMBER 21, 2009

THE HONORABLE MARK WARNER

THE HONORABLE JIM WEBB

RE: FEDERAL HEALTHCARE REFORM LEGISLATION

DEAR SENATORS WARNER AND WEBB:

I HAVE BEEN FOLLOWING WITH GREAT INTEREST THE IMPORTANT DEBATE CURRENTLY TAKING PLACE IN WASHINGTON WITH RESPECT TO THE PROPOSED REFORM OF OUR NATION'S HEALTHCARE SYSTEM.

WHILE I CERTAINLY AGREE THAT WE FACE SERIOUS PROBLEMS WITH RESPECT TO THE AFFORDABILITY AND AVAILABILITY OF HEALTHCARE FOR MANY AMERICANS, IT IS IMPORTANT THAT ANY REFORM LEGISLATION ADDRESS THESE ISSUES WITHOUT CREATING OTHER PROBLEMS FOR AMERICAN CONSUMERS AND BUSINESSES OR JEOPARDIZING THE QUALITY OF OUR HEALTHCARE DELIVERY SYSTEM, WHICH IS CURRENTLY THE BEST IN THE WORLD.

FOR MANY REASONS, I STRONGLY OPPOSE THE HEALTHCARE REFORM LEGISLATION THAT IS CURRENTLY PENDING BEFORE THE UNITED STATES SENATE, AND I ENCOURAGE YOU TO VOTE AGAINST THIS LEGISLATION AND ANY PROCEDURAL VOTES THAT WOULD ALLOW THIS LEGISLATION TO COME TO A FINAL VOTE.

IN MY JUDGMENT, THE LEGISLATION CURRENTLY PENDING IN THE SENATE WILL ULTIMATELY INCREASE THE COST OF HEALTHCARE AND RESULT IN HIGHER HEALTH INSURANCE PREMIUMS AND HIGHER TAXES FOR THE VAST MAJORITY OF THE AMERICAN PEOPLE.

IN ADDITION, I BELIEVE THAT THIS LEGISLATION WILL JEOPARDIZE THE QUALITY OF HEALTHCARE THAT IS CURRENTLY AVAILABLE IN OUR COUNTRY AND TAKE IMPORTANT HEALTHCARE DECISIONS OUT OF THE HANDS OF CONSUMERS AND TURN THESE DECISIONS OVER TO GOVERNMENT BUREAUCRATS.

PERHAPS MOST IMPORTANTLY, I AM CONCERNED THAT THE COST OF THIS LEGISLATION WILL BE MUCH HIGHER THAN CURRENTLY ESTIMATED, AND IT WILL INEVITABLY ADD SIGNIFICANTLY TO OUR FEDERAL GOVERNMENT'S DEFICIT, WHICH IS, QUITE FRANKLY, OUT OF CONTROL AND THREATENS THE LONG TERM FINANCIAL VIABILITY OF OUR NATION.

IF THESE CONCERNS WERE NOT REASON ENOUGH TO VOTE AGAINST THIS MISGUIDED LEGISLATION, I AM WRITING TO YOU TODAY TO LET YOU KNOW THAT I AM OUTRAGED BY REPORTS THAT SURFACED THIS WEEKEND REGARDING CONCESSIONS THAT WERE MADE TO NEBRASKA SENATOR BEN NELSON TO SECURE HIS VOTE IN SUPPORT OF THIS LEGISLATION.

AS YOU KNOW, ONE OF OUR MAJOR CONCERNS WITH THIS LEGISLATION IS THE POTENTIAL IMPACT IT COULD HAVE ON THE COST OF MEDICAID FOR VIRGINIA'S STATE GOVERNMENT. MANY REPORTS HAVE SUGGESTED THAT THIS LEGISLATION COULD RESULT IN MUCH HIGHER MEDICAID COSTS FOR STATE GOVERNMENTS ACROSS THE NATION, COSTS THAT STATE GOVERNMENTS SIMPLY CANNOT BEAR.

AGAINST THIS BACKGROUND, I WAS AMAZED TO HEAR THAT THE SENATE'S DEMOCRATIC LEADERSHIP HAD MADE CONCESSIONS TO SENATOR NELSON THAT WOULD HOLD HIS HOME STATE OF NEBRASKA HARMLESS AS TO ANY ADDITIONAL MEDICAID COSTS THAT MIGHT COME ABOUT AS A RESULT OF THE ENROLLMENT OF NEW MEDICAID RECIPIENTS AFTER 2017.

I FIND THESE REPORTS PARTICULARLY TROUBLING SINCE THEY COME ON THE HEELS OF SIMILAR CONCESSIONS THAT WERE GIVEN TO

SENATOR MARY LANDRIEU OF LOUISIANA TO SECURE HER VOTE IN SUPPORT OF THIS LEGISLATION JUST A FEW WEEKS AGO.

IN ADDITION TO THE "PAY OFFS" THAT WERE OFFERED TO SENATORS NELSON AND LANDRIEU, UNCONFIRMED MEDIA REPORTS OVER THE WEEKEND HAVE REVEALED THAT OTHER SENATORS MAY HAVE NEGOTIATED SIMILAR SPECIAL TREATMENT DEALS FOR THEIR STATES. IF THESE REPORTS ARE ACCURATE, THIS TYPE OF QUID PRO QUO IS UNACCEPTABLE, AND YOU AND YOUR COLLEAGUES SHOULD OBJECT STRONGLY TO THE PRACTICE, WHICH I HAVE NO DOUBT THE AMERICAN PEOPLE WILL FIND OFFENSIVE AS WELL.

IF THE SENATE'S LEADERSHIP IS SO DESPERATE TO OBTAIN VOTES TO SECURE THE PASSAGE OF THIS LEGISLATION THAT THEY WOULD MAKE THESE TYPES OF CONCESSIONS TO THESE SENATORS, I WOULD ASK THAT YOU DEMAND THAT THE SAME CONCESSIONS BE EXTENDED TO VIRGINIA, AND FOR THAT MATTER, TO EVERY OTHER STATE IN THE NATION.

ALLOWING KEY PROVISIONS IN THIS LEGISLATION TO BE USED TO ESSENTIALLY BUY VOTES FROM SENATORS LANDRIEU AND NELSON AT THE EXPENSE OF OTHER STATES SUCH AS VIRGINIA SHOULD BE AS OFFENSIVE TO YOU AS IT IS TO ME, AND IT SHOULD GIVE YOU ALL THE REASON YOU NEED TO OPPOSE THIS MISGUIDED LEGISLATION.

THANK YOU FOR YOUR SERVICE TO THE PEOPLE OF VIRGINIA AND FOR CONSIDERING MY VIEWS ON THIS IMPORTANT ISSUE.

VERY TRULY YOURS,

WILLIAM T. BOLLING

After all of the pleas by the Governors and the people of Virginia, and despite having not read the bill in its entirety in the first place, both Senators voted in favor of the "Patient Protection and Affordability Care Act" (PPACA). If they did understand the financial obligation to their state and the erosion of their state's constitutional protections, they did it in direct violation of their oath of office to be the voice of the state and not of the people or of a party.

As a result of their vote Jim Webb determined that his re-election in 2012 is not viable and has chosen not to run. Mark Warner won't be up for re-election until 2014, and he's certain to make a determination of the viability of his re-election run closer to that timeframe, but I'm certain that it's his hope now, that the people forget his vote or that the law is stricken by the Supreme Court effectively taking him off the hook for his ill-advised vote. Even so, he must know that his yes vote will be used as a reminder to voters that he's looking out for the Democratic Party and not Virginians.

Senators were originally elected by state legislatures according to Article 1, section 3 of the Constitution, to provide the protection of states rights; minimizing the risk that federal powers would attempt to interfere in state business. This would ensure that the federal government kept to their original mandate of national protection, mediation of commerce and the delivery of the mail. Nothing more or less.

When the 17th Amendment was enacted in 1913, the protection of states' rights was effectively removed, and the progression of centralized controls began; over time its culminated into the massive federal government we have today, that has no regard for states' rights, as was demonstrated by Democrats when they blatantly ignored the requests of their respective state legislative bodies and Governors to vote no on the PPACA.

Before the 17th Amendment was enacted, Senators would've been subject to the will of the state or face being replaced when their six year term had expired by the state legislature. There would've been no campaigning, no need for a primary election, just a vote in the state legislature to replace that Senator. Now the states no longer have the ability to protect their rights nor the rights of the citizens of their state; because they have no control over the election of Senators; effectively removing their voice at the table of checks and balances.

It is more than plausible that had we kept the original design our founders created for the balance of powers that Obamacare and a whole host of other laws increasing the size and scope of centralized control in Washington D.C. may not have ever become an issue; because they likely would've never been attempted. The digression of freedom and the growth of the federal government have been by design, and if we take a look at history once again, we see a pattern in the last 112 years. It's not just been Democrats; but many Republicans have been the source of the same expansion and acceptance of the erosion of the Constitution and our freedom.

With the emersion of the two party system of the late 1800's, we became locked in a battle between voting for the lessor of two evils. We either vote for the party who wants to socialize medicine outright or the party that just wants it to become interstate commerce and regulated federally by the commerce clause; either way we are losing our freedoms as citizens to define our own destinies (remember our inalienable rights to life, liberty and the pursuit of happiness, the more laws we allow to be created the less happiness there is to pursue). All this, while the free market is handcuffed with regulations and approvals making it difficult, and in some states impossible, to meet market needs or provide new solutions to the new problems our citizens face today. The bottom line, this cannot be allowed to continue as the status quo.

It's time that we take a stand as freedom loving Americans and chart our own course by getting the federal government out of the business of our business and once again let the Entrepreneurial spirit of the American people solve these problems. This is what has always made America the exception but if we continue down this road to bigger government, our exceptionalism will be replaced; the only question would be replaced with what?

The good news is we are still in a position to choose by voting out those who continue the government expansion model and replace them with Americans who want to see American exceptionalism returned. Over time we will begin to see the swelling of the federal government subside and then shrink back to its original directives of protecting freedom and creating the conditions for the innovation and drive of the American spirit to thrive.

Chapter 3

Obamacare: Socializing American Healthcare

With the enactment of the Patient Protection and Affordable Care Act (PPACA), Congress is imposing a mandate on citizens, effective January 1, 2014, to purchase a federally approved level of health insurance. 2. Federally approved health insurance can be found in Patient Protection and Affordable Care Act of 2010, Public Law 111–148, and Health Care and Education Reconciliation Act of 2010, Public Law 111–152.

The fact that all insurance must meet a federally approved standard is, unarguably, government control of free market health insurance, and it's through that control they indirectly gain control of all our healthcare. Although it's done by writing rules through the Health and Human Services department of the government, every aspect of our coverage will be controlled by politics and bureaucrats. These mandates are the danger because Congress has no oversight authority over the rules process as costs fail to decline in spite of this legislation, HHS can write mandates to control premium costs for re-election purposes. No, no danger in that right?

Premium fixing is nearly a guarantee because politicians are going to use rising costs of healthcare and insurance as political slogans for why we need change. They'll be voted in on their promises, and once they get into office, try to fix it in their first term, fail, then blame it on the opposition party; then promise that if we vote more of their party into Congress, that they can get something done only to disappoint us all in their second term when they have no re-election concerns, it's always the same. But, as costs go up and politicians try to keep the public happy by trying to keep premiums low, a sacrifice in care will have to be made to control costs, there'll be no way around it, under Obamacare its inevitable and maybe even intended.

Secondly, the individual and employer mandates in this plan are based on the political theory that if everyone participates in the forced purchase of medical insurance or pay an imposed penalty, for non-participation, that somehow they can control costs. In fact, not only is there no evidence that this theory will prove true, all evidence points to the contrary.

However, instead of rehashing old arguments about whether this will or won't result in lowering costs; let's apply simple, common sense to the issue. The number that was touted by the Administration during the run up to vote on healthcare reform was somewhere between 30 and 46 million Americans who are without health insurance because of pricing or preexisting condition restrictions.

Common Sense: A simple Google search reveals that the total population of the United States is approximately 313 Million. Although 30 Million uninsured was the number at the time of the debate that number was eventually recalculated up to 46 million according to FactCheck.org 3; that would make the total of uninsured less than 15% of the total population; but if, in fact, the number is 30 million uninsured, it would be less than 10%. Can someone please tell me how forcing 15% more people to buy insurance will bring the cost of the insurance of the 85% down to a reasonable level? If it did impact the premium, it would be an unnoticeable difference.

The truth is that increasing the client base of an insurance company by only 15% will have an insignificant impact on the actuarial tables and premium pricing. It may, though not likely, lower premiums slightly at best, BUT then we're faced with another issue that would be created by the addition of the uninsured with pre-existing conditions.

Common Sense: If we add 46 million people to the roles of the insured and just 10% of those had pre-existing conditions that required some sort of immediate medical treatment or extended care; that's 4.6 million people that would have to be absorbed into the actuarial estimates and eventually the premium calculations. From the insurers perspective, if the average claim paid for each of the newly insured with pre-existing conditions was just $100,000, the total cost to cover them all, would start at $460 Billion. Now can someone please explain with any rational explanation how the insurance companies could absorb $460 Billion dollars in additional upfront costs, and our premiums go down at the same time?

Common Sense: How does spending over one TRILLION dollars to create a new centrally controlled healthcare system make healthcare more affordable? Especially when it creates a mass of new taxes, punishes those who do not want a full healthcare plan, with taxes disguised as penalties; not to mention the number of man hours that businesses would have to pay, just to stay in compliance. At the time of this writing, it was reported that the business community had already seen an increase in costs related to compliance of healthcare reform of roughly 5% in a survey conduct by Willis Group Holdings P.L.C.

Even more telling is a report by several news outlets and others, that the Congressional Budget Office had doubled the costs estimate of the law over the next ten years to $1.76 Trillion 4 before it was "revised" down within hours to $1.1 Trillion. No matter the disparity; one trillion or two means that, the American people have to fund that expense and not one politician can say that we can do that without eventually raising taxes, or borrowing so much money from China that we either become Chinese or default, just like Greece. If we do simple math taking $1 Trillion divided by the population of 313 Million we arrive at an additional tax burden of each person of over $31,000 just to pay for the set up of this plan, but nearly one half of Americans pay absolutely no taxes at all, leaving the burden to be carried by the taxpaying public which doubles their tax burden to approximately $62,000. A family of four with taxpaying parents would be on the hook for nearly $250,000; that's just ridiculous.

More Common Sense: If we add 46 million to the insured population by the wave of the pen with many of our doctors at maximum patient loads (doctor to patient ratio) then who will treat the additional patients created by this law?

Common Sense: Another major issue that was debated at the time was the participation of the illegal immigrant population in American which is estimated to be somewhere between 12 and 20 million people. According to ProCon.org 5 illegal immigrants will NOT be able to purchase health insurance through the insurance exchanges that are required by PPACA. Will the exclusion of their participation in the law prevent them from getting medical care? Or will we still have to pay for their care the same way we do now…out of our taxes?

Other common sense questions: If they are just passing a law that requires all Americans to purchase health insurance from a private company through an insurance exchange that is set up by the states; why is it going to cost tax payers' 1 to 2 Trillion dollars? And why are they taking $500 billion out of Medicare and transferring it to Obamacare? Hmmm, I think these question need to be answered by those who voted yes, without reading the bill first, don't you?

The reason that they pushed this bill through without regard to common sense and in the face of overwhelming opposition by the American people is the same reason we have Social Security today; there's been a movement in

America since the early 1900's toward a socialist style government, that gave us the beginnings of the progressive tax code, Social Security (which isn't so secure today) and Medicare on the federal level. We all know that these programs are leading this country towards bankruptcy. The American people seem to have lost interest in holding politicians accountable, and politicians haven't gotten the courage to shift away from government control or its entitlement programs. Now that Obamacare has passed, it will take the Supreme Court ruling it unconstitutional or politicians with pure political will to repeal it (yeah, like that'll happen). One thing is for certain though; as we've seen with all other government entitlements: this one will also cost far more than projected and will inflict further damage to the strength of our economy and diminish our freedoms, of that we can be certain.

The other reason they pushed so hard to pass this bill, and in my view the more sinister plot, is to move us toward a single payer system which is what President Obama and several of the Congressional leaders plainly stated they wanted. Speaking in front of his supporters at an AFL-CIO event, President Obama not only states that he's a proponent of universal healthcare, he specifies that he means a single payer system, and that once they'd won the

White House and Congress, that he would push for a single payer system in America. So it's irrefutable that our President's preference is a single payer universal healthcare system despite the political rhetoric of today.

If it's not been scrubbed by the release of this book, you can see Mr. Obama in his own words here: http://youtu.be/fpAyan1fXCE

However, he's not alone in that desire; if you recall during these debates Speaker Nancy Pelosi and the Democrats in the House pushed and passed healthcare reform that included a "public option". But Barney Frank in a brief interview was clear that the intention of the public option was, that it would eventually lead to a single payer system.

See it for yourself: http://youtu.be/JoU1r3segmo

There are many other advocates of a single payer healthcare system, just to name a few that have gone on record:

Dennis Kucinich, Maxine Waters and Russ Feingold but we can add every politician to vote yes on the House version of healthcare reform and I would suggest that most of the Senators who voted yes on the Senate version.

With this clear understanding of the original intent of our elected officials, we now get a better picture of what they've been planning behind closed doors, the type of healthcare they prefer and the direction they want to take America. Although they failed to pass the public option in the Senate, the end game is the same, a single payer universal healthcare system. Because of the unpopularity of an open vote for the public option, the Senate had to change their strategy slightly but the end game is the very same and they have a plan to get back on track.

If you recall, they pushed hard and ultimately rushed to pass the Senate version of the bill in the House, which had previously been denounced by many congressmen and women as ineffective legislation because it didn't include the public options, before they finally voted yes. It was even said to be ineffective by Candidate Obama in debates with Hilary Clinton 6 so, if you these politicians knew that the individual mandate wouldn't work, why did they vote yes. Seemed odd, didn't it?

The point is they had a supermajority, and if Democrats believed that the plan with a public option was the best plan for America, why did they ultimately agree to the Senate bill which simply mandated coverage? The answer is simple, they just needed to get a program started that required massive government involvement, and I personally believe they have their intentions are to make major modifications to that program in the years to come to gain even more control. My personal beliefs aside, one thing is clear, the possibilities for ideological intentions toward a single payer system are built into even the Senate bill and here's how it can work for them.

The Department of Health and Human Services Director, currently Kathleen Sebelius, who is also a proponent of a single payer system, will write the rules by which insurance companies, who participate in the insurance exchanges, are required to follow. In an article, by US News 7, 6 pages of the PPACA is equivalent to 426 pages of new rules that must be followed, that's a total of approximately 191,700 new rules!

In just the last few months, we've seen what this really means. When the department wrote a rule requiring all private health insurers must cover contraception including the 'week after pill' which has been reported to potentially cause abortions. Then they told all employers, including religious ones, that the healthcare they provide to their employees also must provide these same contraception, even in the face of religious objection to contraception.

The Hill reported:

"UNTIL NOW," SAID ROMAN CATHOLIC ARCHDIOCESE OF WASHINGTON CHANCELLOR JANE BELFORD, "FEDERAL LAW HAS NEVER PREVENTED RELIGIOUS EMPLOYERS ... FROM PROVIDING FOR THE NEEDS OF THEIR EMPLOYEES WITH A HEALTH PLAN THAT IS CONSISTENT WITH THE CHURCH'S MORAL TEACHINGS. THIS WOULD CHANGE UNDER THE HHS MANDATE."

Just as objectionable the HHS could write rules forcing insurers to cover "women's health issues" (which is code word for abortion) and in this interview 8 it would seem that's the plan of the current HHS director, Kathleen Sebelius. She stated that current law prohibits federal funds from being used for reproductive rights of women with a few exceptions; and the Senate bill, which was negotiated by Barbara Boxer and Patty Murray, (who are women's rights advocates), would maintain that standard.

The end right?… well, not so fast. She goes on to say "making sure there are some plan options for women"; well what exactly does that mean? She goes on to clarify: "while making sure that public funds aren't used, we are not isolating against, discriminate against or invading the privacy rights of women" and how exactly would they do that? Kathleen Sebelius explains, "It would be an accounting procedure, but everybody in the exchange would do the same whether you're male or female, whether you're 75 or 25 you'd all set aside a portion of your premium that would go into a fund; it wouldn't be earmarked for anything", she says, "but it would be a separate account". After the interviewer states that it's confusing, she clarifies her statement saying, "It is a bit confusing, but it's really an accounting measure that would apply across the board, not just to women and certainly not just to women who want to choose abortion coverage". The bottom line, this Secretary will find a way to provide abortion options to women by simply writing a mandate.

See the interview for yourself: http://youtu.be/uCmFFDyDrv8

Late on Friday, March 16th 2012, it was reported by the New York Times the clarification of the mandate that would force employers (including religious employers who object that the coverage) contraception would be provided for women by someone, writing:

THE OBAMA ADMINISTRATION TOOK ANOTHER STEP ON FRIDAY TO ENFORCE A FEDERAL MANDATE FOR HEALTH INSURANCE COVERAGE

OF CONTRACEPTIVES, ANNOUNCING HOW THE NEW REQUIREMENT WOULD APPLY TO THE MANY ROMAN CATHOLIC HOSPITALS, UNIVERSITIES AND SOCIAL SERVICE AGENCIES THAT INSURE THEMSELVES.

IN SUCH CASES, THE ADMINISTRATION SAID, FEMALE EMPLOYEES AND STUDENTS WILL STILL HAVE ACCESS TO FREE COVERAGE OF CONTRACEPTIVES.

THE COVERAGE WILL BE PROVIDED BY THE COMPANIES THAT REVIEW AND PAY CLAIMS — "THIRD-PARTY ADMINISTRATORS" — OR BY "SOME OTHER INDEPENDENT ENTITY," IT SAID.

My previous statements are proving true on a regular basis; the Health and Human Services Secretary is writing rules that force an ideological position on those of us who conscientiously object as a matter of our religious beliefs; because their definition of contraception includes abortifacient drugs that can and are used to induce abortions.

Oh, it's just an accounting measure…right? Why would you use an accounting procedure to put funds into a separate account, if it wasn't for a specific reason? In this case, that reason was clearly explained by Kathleen Sebelius…it's for abortions.

By setting aside funds in a separate account (thereby, earmarking premiums) that are to be used to provide "women's health and reproductive rights" options, you are forcing the funding of abortions on those who are pro-life. So in other words, they can't use tax payer money but will use a portion of the premium dollars paid to insurers through the federally regulated and mandated exchanges to force those who oppose abortion to fund it...period, and that goes against freedom first of all, and so many Americans conscience, not just Catholics. It's a clear violation of our First Amendment rights to freedom of religion, because a right to life is a religious position, not a political one.

In the same interview, she also stated that insurers for the first time will be required to report their medical loss ratios to HHS. As of January 1, 2011, health insurance issuers are now required spend at least 80% of the premium dollars they receive, from selling policies and plans in the individual market, and at least 80% from policies they sell in the small group market, on a combination of medical care claims and activities to improve health care quality. The parallel rule for the large group market (more than 50 employees) requires an 85% expenditure. Effectively, the MLR provision limits the amount that insurers can spend on administrative expense, overhead, profit, commissions, and other non-claim expenses to just 15% or 20% of the premium. This is government control at its finest.

Listen, we could go on for days about the HHS socializing our healthcare system through the rules process instead of the legislative process. The bottom line is that these types of bureaucratic rules will serve only to provide burdensome paperwork and additional man power to stay in compliance with the HHS rules increasing costs to the insurer and ultimately the consumer, unless HHS prevents premiums increases.

When administration and claims costs rise, the insurers will petition the HHS to increase premiums (as will be required by the rules) to make up for the loss in profitability. The only thing the HHS Secretary, who has complete authority over every aspect of the insurance exchanges, has to do… is say No!

In order to achieve a single payer system all that would be required under this new rules process, is to keep slowly suffocating insurers with burdensome rules and profit containment measures to weed out the smaller insurers who will be unable to keep us with compliance. As the insurers opt out of the exchanges, the larger insurers will take control of existing policies until just a few insurers are left or one of them lobbies the right politicians and gains control of all the policies within the exchange leaving us with…that's right folks, a single payer system with the caveat of an insurance company who is the single payer but is controlled by the federal government via the HHS.

Not to mention the other politics that will be used; just like with Medicare and Social Security which are quite literally bankrupting our country. Most politicians use these programs to play political games, in an attempt to make the other party look like they hate grandma and grandpa, and want to expedite their demise; even when one of them offers legitimate options to ensure its solvency, its opposition is used for some kind of political game. To watch it gives me a headache, but, to me, it seems like if the opposing party didn't think of it, then it's like they're require by the party code to object, all while the country is swirling in the toilet bowl, it's just stupid. The same will be done with Obamacare and deep down we all know it.

Now, think about it; the Secretary of HHS is appointed by the Administration and will change as new administrations come and go; this creates a constantly changing regulatory climate that insurers will have to continually, modify policies provisions and exclusions to accommodate political pressures. This will consistently add administrative costs to the insurer, further, diminishing the profitability of all the insurers included in the exchanges; or if allowed, increase our premiums.

Over time with continued resistance by the American public to premium increases; politics, instead of market principles, take over and dictate that no or very modest premium increases will be allowed just as we've seen with the post office and Medicare; when was the last time they raised the Medicare payroll tax? The only difference being that Congress will have absolutely no oversight authority in this case… it'll just be one person at HHS; the Secretary, and whomever they assign to help… that's it, no one else.

Imagine this reality; we elect a new President who wants his constituents to be happy with his performance. With a phone call to the newly appointed HHS Secretary, he can have them "mandate" lower premiums for consumers. Although consumers may be happy with the action, the result will be disastrous as mounting pressure forces more and more insurers to back out of the exchanges, and go it alone in an attempt to maintain a profitable business model.

Under that scenario, if administrations were to continue to ignore the real issues with our health costs but instead target the profit of insurers as a means to lower premiums to consumers; they will, whether intentional or not, cause the collapse of the industry as a whole. Leaving the government with "no choice" but to pull the administration of all the policies in the insurance exchange, in house, effectively eliminating private healthcare coverage for the foreseeable future.

Both of these outcomes are unacceptable and lead to the same result; government's continued and direct intervention and control of our medical industry and ultimately our freedom of choice over our health. And don't think that once the exchanges fail, we'll just go back to the way things were! By that time, the employer delivery of health insurance will have been virtually destroyed. Why you ask?

This law has created the conditions to encourage businesses to opt out of the employer sponsored delivery of health insurance by making it far less expensive for employers to pay the fine in lieu of providing insurance to their employees. An employer who doesn't offer the federally approved health insurance to their employees will be fined

$2,000 per employee, BUT they are exempt from the fine on the first 30 employees.

Even without the exemption $2,000 per year is a less costly and a more predictable expense than actually providing the health insurance to employees. As a fiscal bottom line measure, and if you add the exemption; from a business perspective, it would seem a no brainer to pay the fine, as opposed to providing the benefit. Which I believe, has the intended consequence of pushing employees into the insurance exchanges; and if the demise of the employer healthcare delivery system is the intention, then this would be a required effect of the law.

Candidate Obama at a SEIU event 9 stated that the transition from an employer based delivery system, to a single payer system would take about 15 years; there is of course massive debate over the context by which made these statements, and it's been used by both sides for political posturing. However, that's not to say that the timeframe was inaccurate; a 15 year transition is realistic. That amount of time would allow employers to conclude that they can't fight the system, and may as well save the expense. This would push more and more Americans into the insurance exchanges, and that's intended....why?

As we've discussed the HHS department will write the rules for the implementation of Obamacare and how easily the HHS department will be used for political ends just as Medicare and Social Security are today. When too many insurers are forced out of the exchanges to a bare employer based market, the next "healthcare crisis" will emerge giving the government the opportunity to, finally, take control of healthcare. The model for this take over is already a reality in the states, when an insurer becomes insolvent. What happens there is the department of insurance takes control of an insolvent insurance company, including all its policy assets; while they liquidate the insurance company they sell the policies to other insurance companies as a way to protect the consumer from a loss of coverage, and a way to generate funds to pay the insurer's debts.

The possibilities as it relates to the insurance exchanges are that smaller companies will back out, and policies will be absorbed by (sold to) the larger companies; the result: we end up with "competition" of one or two insurers. These companies beholden to the government for their profitability become a private extension of the federal government much like Fanny Mae and Freddy Mac; or worse, another hugely progressive administration wins the

White House and without the need for Congress, appoints another proponent of universal healthcare.

With the stroke of the pen, they write a new rule forcing insurers to reduce premiums by a significant margin. This single act would be incredibly popular with the populace while being the final death blow for the semi-free market of the health insurance industry. When the remaining insurers fail, the government, while proclaiming from the highest podiums in D.C. that through no fault of their own, they have no choice but to take control of all the policies in the exchange to ensure that Americans can continue to have their health issues covered, they'll do just take... take control. And we'll have arrived at what was the original intent of this administration and many others; a single payer, universal healthcare system completely controlled by the federal government.

As you can see, we've explained many different ways the universal healthcare proponents can achieve that end, and they'll do it, while blaming the insurance companies for failing the American people. We better pray that the Supreme Court rules this law unconstitutional in June after having heard the arguments on both sides; otherwise we have a long and rough road ahead of us trying to repeal it, and the longer it takes to repeal this law the steeper the climb to change it back will become. But, right now I wouldn't quite look to the Republicans for a reasonable alternative option either; just a slower one.

Chapter 4

The Republican Alternative That Leads To Controlling Our Healthcare

Although it's true that Obamacare is the most dangerous healthcare plan America has ever seen, and its defeat is paramount to the future success of our country. The GOP under the leadership of John Boehner has passed a resolution to replace President Obama's healthcare reform bill called H.R.2 that won't lead us to a viable solution either. H.R. 2 enacted a 5 point plan (10) that included:

Enact Medical Liability Reform

Skyrocketing medical liability insurance rates have distorted the practice of medicine, routinely forcing doctors to order costly and often unnecessary tests to protect themselves from lawsuits, often referred to as "defensive medicine." We will enact common-sense medical liability reforms to lower costs, rein in junk lawsuits and curb defensive medicine.

Purchase Health Insurance across State Lines

Americans residing in a state with expensive health insurance plans are locked into those plans and do not currently have an opportunity to choose a lower cost option that best meets their needs. We will allow individuals to buy health care coverage outside of the state in which they live.

Expand Health Savings Accounts

Health Savings Accounts (HSAs) are popular savings accounts that provide cost effective health insurance to those who might otherwise go uninsured. We will improve HSAs by making it easier for patients with high-deductible health plans to use them to obtain access to quality care. We will repeal the new health care law, which prevents the use of these savings accounts to purchase over-the-counter medicine.

Ensure Access for Patients with Pre-Existing Conditions

Health care should be accessible for all, regardless of pre-existing conditions or past illnesses. We will expand state high-risk pools, reinsurance programs and reduce the cost of coverage. We will make it illegal for an insurance company to deny coverage to someone with prior coverage on the basis of a pre-existing condition, eliminate annual and lifetime spending caps, and prevent insurers from dropping your coverage just because you get sick. We will incentivize states to develop innovative programs that lower premiums and reduce the number of uninsured Americans.

Permanently Prohibit Taxpayer Funding of Abortion

We will establish a government-wide prohibition on taxpayer funding of abortion and subsidies for insurance coverage that includes abortion. This prohibition would go further and enact into law what is known as the Hyde Amendment, as well as ban other instances of federal subsidies for abortion services. We will also enact into law conscience protections for health care providers, including doctors, nurses, and hospitals.

While there are some good aspects to this plan, like medical liability reform (A.K.A. Tort Reform), for example, and helping those with pre-existing conditions; of course, I personally like the prevention of abortion funding, it still leads us to a slightly less intrusive version of federal government control of our healthcare, but it's still government control. The aspect of their reform that will, in fact, do harm to a viable solution to healthcare costs is the purchase of healthcare across state lines.

Why? Just like Obamacare it gives control over health insurers to the federal government and most prominently the HHS department, which leads to the same regulation through mandates.

How: There is a good reason that insurance isn't sold across state lines and it's called the commerce clause. Since the creation of health insurance, states knew and still know that regulation of such a personal decision should be kept within its borders. They've always known that if the federal government could control our healthcare it would gladly take that control. Through the commerce clause, the HHS would make cookie cutter mandates and regulations that might be applicable to New York residence but might not work in Arizona or vice versa.

The minute insurance in sold across state lines the federal government takes over jurisdiction of the regulation of every health insurance product sold in the United States. That is a power that was granted to them under the Constitution and they are more than happy to have that control. Not to sound the alarm or anything, but that has just as much potential of ending at a single payer or limited payer system as Obamacare; because just like Obamacare the HHS department would write the rules for insurance companies. Don't think so?

Just to point out another freedom granted to us in the Constitution that has since been limited under the "commerce clause".

Have you ever heard of the National Firearms Act of 1934? Under this act, the federal government substantially taxed certain weapons that they deemed "gangster weapons" as a means to control their purchase. That power was granted them in the Constitution under; you guessed it, the commerce clause.

There was a time in America that you could purchase and carry a firearm without federal government involvement, but as it is with the government when given the opportunity to gain control, any control, they'll take it, along with more freedom than they otherwise are entitled to. And, just like firearms, healthcare will be no different if they are given the authority to regulate it; mark my words.

Think about it this way; the same argument that is being currently posed against Obamacare can authentically be levied against GOP solution of cross state line purchases. Now I understand that it wouldn't be to the scale or as blatant as Obamacare is, but has too much potential to end in the same place.

We all know that, at some point, there's going to be some disparity between states over some policy or other provisions and it's guaranteed to become an issue in regards to state taxing of insurance policies being sold across state lines. As it's currently structured, the states collect taxes on the sale of insurance products sold within their states. If we open the borders a bone of contention between states is built into the solution, and when that happens, the federal government, under the commerce clause of the Constitution, will have to step in and mitigate the problems and create laws or rules to deal with all these issues. It's what they do best!

Say, for example, Louisiana's health insurers offer the nation the best rates for the benefit dollar; people from all over the country purchase their insurance from them and not their resident state. There will be lawsuits filed for the tax revenue being generated by Louisiana and lost by the other states. Not to mention, it would also cause an actuarial firestorm and become unmanageable except by the largest insurance companies; smaller companies would lose their competitive edge and that would reduce the competition in the marketplace which is the exact opposite effect that they're intending. Ultimately, other than the dramatic price tag of Obamacare, we are stuck with two boats to choose from and both are listing; one with a one foot hole and the other a ten foot hole; the question is how fast we want to sink the industry with these options.

Over time, more problems will present themselves with health insurance and more federal regulations will be needed to solve those problems. And as we've seen with the government's creation of a "healthcare crisis", but didn't in fact, exist. The vision cast by our public servants, of people left to die in the streets if we didn't quickly pass the healthcare reform measures. This is what we must remember before we decide if we should travel the road to any government control as an alternative to a true free market solution.

The reality is that the GOP solution doesn't address the primary cost drivers in a direct and purposeful way, which would have any dramatic impact; in the end, it's exactly as the picture describing their solution…a Band-Aid and we all know the problem is bigger than a Band-Aid can fix. Our healthcare costs need to be addressed with bold ideas, because we can no longer afford to patch the system, when it needs a completely new strategy.

We can and we must do much more as Americans to solve our problem with health costs. Leaving it to politicians and bureaucrats to be thoughtful and effective enough to create the solutions, is just asking for more pain; and frankly their treatments are worse than the disease. Let's face it, no matter which party you claim allegiance to or favor, neither are more capable of producing solutions than the driving force of the American entrepreneur, who has the capability and reason, to actually solve this problem.

We need ideas; big ones, and I'm going to present my ideas in the hopes of sparking a new conversation about what Americans can do within their own communities, to remove the need for a government solution all together. Because government solutions only lead to government control; government control has never proven to reduce the costs of anything in America; that's why we pay so much for our national defense, our educational system is a mess and every agency of the government is bloated.

As Thomas Jefferson once said, *"The states can best govern our home concerns, and the [federal] government our foreign ones."*

The bottom line is the people closest to the problem are the solution to this challenge; so let's get to work solving this problem.

Chapter 5

The Lie Being Told About Insurance Companies

Far too many Americans believe, and the media has perpetuated this myth, that an insurance companies' profit margin is much greater that is actually the case. Insurers have a 3% profit margin but are marginalized by politicians and others, while companies like Coca Cola who posted an 18% profit margin in September of 2011, at least for now, are overlooked. Why single out health insurers who are already operating at as low a profit margin as 3%?

A government who singles out entire industries for special treatment whether in favor of or against is too powerful for freedom to prevail and must be downsized before all is lost.

I regretfully admit, that I used to be a smoker (not that I recommend smoking, but it was my choice to smoke) and I can remember when I could buy a carton of name brand cigarettes for about $10; but for years, the government had targeted the industry because it had been proven that smoking could lead to cancer. First they couldn't advertise, and then they had to label each pack of smokes with the infamous and now common Surgeon General's Warning.

The industry complied but did the scrutiny stop there... oh no.

In 1999, the government determined that healthcare costs for smokers were higher than non-smokers and was causing the increase in costs and rises in health insurance premiums for the entire market. So, the Clinton Administration announced during the 1999 State of the Union address that he would direct his Justice Department to prepare litigation against tobacco companies to pay for the increased expenses paid by Medicare, Medicaid and other federal programs.

That was brought about because in June, 1998 a Jacksonville Florida jury ordered Brown & Williamson

Tobacco Company to pay almost $1 million to the family of Roland Maddox, who died of lung cancer after 48 years of smoking Lucky Strike cigarettes. His family sued, claiming the company was negligent; made a defective product and conspired with other tobacco companies, to hide the health risks of smoking from the public.

From that day on the tobacco industry was left alone.

Not a chance; the Obama Administration on February 4, 2009, went forward with the Children's Health Insurance Program Reauthorization Act of 2009, which was signed into law. It raised the federal tax rate for cigarettes on April 1, 2009 from $0.39 per pack to $1.01 per pack. This act also included the requirement for graphic images to be placed on each pack. Companies, led by R.J. Reynolds Tobacco and Lorillard Tobacco Companies, sued the FDA to block the labels, arguing the labels cross the line from fact-based warnings to anti-smoking advocacy.

Now before I irritate some who may read this; I am not promoting smoking to anyone. As a former smoker, I understand that it can make people sick and can cause death. My grandfather died from emphysema brought on by a lifetime of smoking, so I truly understand the effects of smoking. But people have a choice to smoke and to quit, and I finally did and if someone doesn't shouldn't they responsible for their own actions if they already know the risks?

The question that needs to be asked; if the Health and Human Services director is the sole authority over the insurance exchanges and a trend is reported that Americans are eating too many hamburgers, and it's causing illness and even death through heart disease, couldn't the same logic that was used to successfully sue the tobacco companies be levied against, say McDonalds? It will only take one successful lawsuit against the mega burger company to set a legal precedent for the government to then, sue the fast food industry for lying to the public and making a defective product; and then let the taxation begin to "pay for the increased expense of healthcare". Imagine paying $10 for a happy meal or the quarter pounder being replaced by the quarter McVeganburger or some other ridiculous thing.

You see where I'm headed with this… right?; although it may be very easy to label the tobacco industry as evil and in many respects that may be true; but in the hands of a government institution looking to justify their existence, it would be far too easy for them to take aim at any industry for nearly any reason…too much salt, too much sugar and everyone's current favorite evil foods with too much fat. You get the point.

If you don't believe that the tendency of the government is to control its citizens, then try this story on for size. A four year old girl brought a bagged lunch to school that had a turkey sandwich, a banana, chips and an apple juice that was taken from her by an unidentified inspector who told her the lunch wasn't healthy enough. The girl went home with a bill for $1.25 for a replacement lunch that was given to her. 11.

It's obvious, when the government thinks it can control our healthcare then the progression to other aspects of our lives is a fairly easy transition. What we eat will become a public health concern dooming the businesses that won't comply with the government's standards of healthy eating. As the story above shows, it's already starting.

We should all disagree with punishing an entire industry for the personal choices of individuals after they've been properly informed of the risks of their behavior. The government has a responsibility to expose and punish illegal actions. But they exposed the tobacco companies who were hiding facts about the dangers and addictiveness of smoking and punished those who intentionally misled the public, but it still hasn't ended there. The government was right to warn citizens of the risks of smoking and even to make tobacco companies warn buyers of the potential risks; but that's where it should've stopped. As a result of the aggressive tactics of the government singling out the tobacco industry; consumers are now spending nearly $50 or more per carton for name brand cigarettes; because the tobacco companies just passed the increased cost of operations and the tax burden onto the consumer. So really, it's the very people of whom the government is claiming they are protecting who are made to pay the government's price for being an evil company; not the tobacco companies.

I know that I'm going to take some heat for using tobacco companies as an example, but they are the clearest example of what happens when government targets an "evil" industry, and why the federal government should never be involved in social programs like medicine, retirement or for that matter anything related to our domestic living.

In the end, we have to look at the reality of what Obamacare and the Republican alternatives would do to the industry, and how that'll affect all of us. Just like the tobacco companies, when government causes a company to spend more to bring a product to market; that cost, whether we like it or not, is and will always be factored into the cost charged to consumers for that product. The only way to avoid that is through governmental price controls which would have an effect on the quality of the product or service that we receive. Frankly, both are undesirable.

I can say that with confidence, because of my personal experience with government controlled medicine. You don't have to look farther than the nearest Veteran and ask them if the care they receive in the Veteran's clinic or hospital is the same quality of care as a private doctor or hospital. In the VA system, every cost is measured, and Congress can add or subtract benefits based on the political winds, with no regard for the wellbeing of our honored servicemen and women.

It was recently reported that President Obama in his budget proposal included a cut in Veterans health benefits by asking active duty, retired and even disabled Veterans to pay more for their healthcare. The Washington Free Beacon reported:

The proposed increases in health care payments by service members, which must be approved by Congress, are part of the Pentagon's $487 billion cut in spending. It seeks to save $1.8 billion from the Tricare medical system in the fiscal 2013 budget, and $12.9 billion by 2017.

This ought to make it easy to understand. If an Administration is willing and able to cut into the healthcare benefits of Veterans, a group of Americans who actually deserve their healthcare from taxpayers, then why wouldn't an Administration who desired to, do the same with Obamacare whether it is the current Administration or a future one?

Not to mention the cost control measures in place, to ensure that the Veterans Administration doesn't exceed their allotted amount of the federal budget. Allow me to share my personal VA story; a couple of years ago I was diagnosed with a skin condition called plaque psoriasis, which I had on my hands. Well, that was after I saw my primary care physician who insisted that I had a fungal infection on my hands and gave me jock itch cream as a treatment. The treatment not only didn't work, but actually made the condition worse—but who can I complain to? When the doctor realized that I didn't have jock itch on my hands but, in fact, needed to see a Dermatologist he put in the referral.

Four months later I had my appointment of which I can say I received good treatment; but the treatment was with medicines that were older, generic ones which only worked for awhile. Some of the other treatments they recommended had side effects that I wasn't willing to risk, like causing birth defects to an unborn child; my wife happened to be pregnant at the time and well let's just say that wasn't a good option for me.

When I happened upon a friend of mine who had the same condition, she gave me a sample of a new medicine she was prescribed by her dermatologist, who, as you may have guessed, is a private doctor. The sample began to work and my condition improved; when I asked to be prescribed that medicine at my VA dermatology clinic, I was told I could get it, but that it had to be approved by the head of the Dermatology department and the VA. This was just a tube of steroidal cream! It may have cost more than the generic ones they wanted me to use, but it did work when the generics didn't.

Now can you imagine getting the approval for the newest Cancer fighting drug? My guess is that process would be much more challenging than the one I experienced. And if I'm not mistaken and I'm not certain, certain care options and drugs are also limited for Medicare and Medicaid patients, as well.

The point is, that government involvement in a free market system that isn't illegal or immoral only increases the cost for all of us and when that cost gets out of control and the government tries to "fix" the problem, they usually cause even more problems than they fix. If anything, the history of all of our social programs we have today, make that point, and rather easily I might add.

The reality is that insurance companies have already reduced their profit margins to what most businesses would consider unsustainable levels; and right now they are being targeted by the government, to include more people, pay out more in claims, all while, we insist they reduce premiums to affordable levels; it's neither doable nor sensible to suggest that it is possible without a dramatic rethinking of the way health costs are covered.

How do we do that?

We start with understanding the real problem because.....

Chapter 6

The Real Problem: Not A Healthcare Crisis; A Health Cost Crisis

What we were told during the "debate", which was really a non-debate because it was one sided (or maybe they meant a debate over bad and worse... yeah that sounds right), anyway, the debate over healthcare reform was that we had a healthcare crisis in America. Now, I would argue that we don't have a health "care" crisis, because all citizens and non-citizens, for that matter, in one way or another, have complete access to health "care". As we've pointed out before 85% or more have health insurance of some kind while others have access through government programs or county clinics and hospitals, and everyone's fallback position is the emergency room, which, not one person in America can be denied medical care because of their inability to pay...period.

Are there inefficiencies in the system we have?

Of course! No system is 100% efficient, but our system is far more efficient than any system that has socialized medicine; I don't care what Danny Glover says, Cuba, give me a break!

The crisis we have in healthcare isn't the method of its delivery, but the cost of that delivery. Now when a normal company runs into issues with high costs, they don't turn to the government and tell them that they need to make more people buy their product because it's causing their consumers to pay more… that in any other industry would be preposterous. No, they identify cost drivers and find ways to reduce those costs to make their product more price competitive and that's what needs to happen with health costs.

So the first step, in solving the problem is to identify the source of that problem, so let's take a look at what that looks like in reality.

One of the things that all businesses must do to remain competitive in any free market is to control costs. When competition comes to market with an equivalent product at a more affordable price, businesses are forced to analyze their cost drivers and work to reduce and sometimes eliminate them, or face going out of business.

The same is true with our personal budgets. If our income is reduced, we have to look at what we're spending our money on, make the decisions to cut back or eliminate some of the luxuries. For example if we are paying $85 per month on cable and we may decide to get the $19.99 per month basic cable or cut cable all together. It really is just common sense.

The truth is that we don't have a healthcare crisis in America because we have government programs like Medicare for the elderly, Medicaid for the poor, Chips for children, the VA Hospitals and clinics for our Veterans and county hospitals for the uninsured. On top of that, every state has laws that force hospitals to treat people regardless of their ability to pay. All of which, I would remind you; taxpayers are picking up the tab for; so again I ask; who doesn't have access to healthcare?

What we have in America is a healthcare cost crisis which is resulting in more and more citizens being pushed out of private health insurance. This is creating a dual problem of people, who are accustomed to having insurance and private doctors, being forced into government programs or county clinics for treatment, and of course, the rising costs to the taxpayers for utilization of these programs.

This problem is going to continue even under Obamacare or the Republican alternative because like our current system, they too, addresses the symptoms of the health cost crisis and not the disease itself; the cost drivers are the disease of our healthcare industry. If we can identify these cost drivers, then we can isolate them and find solutions to each of them, resulting in an overall reduction in the cost of healthcare. It makes sense, doesn't it? So, what are these cost drivers?

Chapter 7

Identify the Real Cost Drivers

We've identified several that we'll discuss here, but I'm certain with more eyes on the problem we could identify many more.

Overuse and improper use of health insurance

If we are going to discuss cost drivers, we have to start with the largest one of them all: claims. According to Blue Cross Blue Shield 87% of all premium dollars are paid out in claims to hospitals, doctors and other health related services. Another 6% goes to pay government fees, compliance and claims processing and administration fees.

So we can't get away from it; the number one cost driver making it expensive to purchase health insurance is the pure volume of claims that are paid by insurers. Like it or not that impacts the cost of the premiums we pay. So, it stands to reason that one of the places to look for savings would be in the claims process or the claims themselves. One of the things that doctors and insurers will tell you, it's the nickel and dime claims that cost the most to process and maintain. Although it's not the fault of patients, what's happened, is an environment has been created that incentivizes the use of insurance over self-payment, which contributes to the overall problem we're currently facing.

The way we arrive at this overuse of health insurance is a societal function and a personal choice. We don't like to be sick, and we want to hurry our bodies back to wellness by getting the best medicines on the market, to address our particular symptoms. So, when we get the sniffles our first response, if it doesn't clear in a day or so, is to call the doctor and set an appointment. Then we go to the doctor only to find out that all we can do is rest and drink lots of liquid; essentially riding it out. Unfortunately, every one of these events creates a billable event for which the doctor and the insurer must spend time, money and effort to process, thus adding to the high volume of claims.

Now, before you get riled up, about how that's why you pay your premium; I want you to know that I agree with you. If an insurance company promises to pay for doctor visits without limitations, then they should pay, and you should see your doctor as often as you like. The point I'm making, is about the pure cost of doing so. In just mathematical terms if every insured person were to see the doctor just once for an otherwise benign reason and the average cost of a doctor visit was $100 then the total cost that must be covered by insurers would be $26.6 Billion. I arrived at that figure by taking the current population estimate of 313 million people times 85% (because the highest estimate of uninsured Americans was 46 million or 15% of the population) times $100. It's that simple.

Now, it should be easier to see why small claims have such a dramatic impact on the overall cost of healthcare premium. It costs insurers approximately the same amount of money to pay a small claim as they do a large one, but they have to carry larger staff to handle the volume, more controls have to be put in place to minimize mistakes and to control fraud. So, you see, the high dollar claims are what insurance should be for, but for these smaller claims, we need a new strategy because they are contributing factors of the overall problem.

That problem, coupled with the perfection we demand of our doctors in their diagnosis, has led them to avoid making any determinations as to the severity of our situation in a non-billable way. What I mean by that is, you can't just call a nurse who'll tell you whether or not your symptoms are concerning enough that the doctor would need to physically see you, which forces us, as patience to make an appointment to see the doctor in person, again creating a billable event to the insurance company. Of course, improper insurance product designs add to the troubles we are currently experiencing with health costs, but we'll talk about that a bit later.

Administration of these claims only serves to add to the problem too. Both the doctor and the insurance company have administrative expenses that affect our premiums. A doctor has to hire trained staff to bill insurance companies for all the services they provide to patients. The insurers have administration costs of staff and systems to receive and process each claim received by doctors and hospitals which is then added to our premiums. Plus insurers also have specialized staff to mitigate losses caused by fraud. And as we all know companies don't ultimately pay any costs; they only pass them on; so every dollar increase in cost is certain to be added to our premiums.

Let's just put it into easy terms, a doctor has to hire a billing specialist who is a person who went to a school to learn how to code, process and file a claim to an insurance company. The average billing specialist earns approximately $30,000 and is most likely offered benefits. All of that cost is added to the doctor's fee, which is charged to the insurance company. All of those fees are paid out as claims by the insurance company, who takes those claims and determines how much they have to charge as premiums in order for them to make a profit of any kind. It's a vicious cycle of fee compilation and we pay for all of it!

There are far more small claims than large ones, and with the costs being nearly identical, claims costs are weighted toward the smaller claims. So, to reduce costs we have to understand that the large claims are necessary and then ask the question whether or not the small ones are; in fact:

The CDC tracks the utilization of health services across the industry and gives estimates every five years or so; the last one came out in April 2011. In that report, it was determined that 48.1% of all the care received in the United States in 2007 was in the primary care physicians offices. Based on that estimate, 48% of all the claims were largely just nickel and dime doctor visits. If we apply that to the national figure of $2.6 Trillion, that means that nearly $1.2 Trillion is paid for primary care services which includes minor injury events or illnesses; within those dollars, there is no way that we couldn't find savings.

But that's from 2007 and you have to rely on government data to come to that conclusion.

As we've attempted to demonstrate so that everyone can see, small claims and administrative costs of those claims drives premium costs up. It's certainly not the only cost driver, but it's a significant one and deserves our attention. In our DocNet solution, we'll demonstrate how to eliminate nearly half of all the claims being submitted to insurers and dramatically reduce the costs of insurance.

Let me demonstrate it in real dollars. If the average American with insurance, that's roughly 267 million (313 million minus the 46 million without coverage), sees the doctor just one time per year for a routine check up at an average cost per visit of $150 for that check up; the total claims cost is over **$40 Billion**. Every dollar of that would be translated into added costs and passed on to us in our premiums.

Two things must be noted here that should be obvious. One, it's not 2007; it's 2012, and I would say that the number of doctor visits has most likely gone up since then. Secondly, we used an average estimated cost of $150, but that is solely dependent on where you live because insurance companies literally determine your premium on your zip code and the average costs charged by doctors per procedure in that area. (I'd go into how that works but trust me; it's a snoozer!)

Our solution removes the small dollars claims for primary and minor medical care services which will dramatically reduce the cost of health insurance premium charged to all of us. How? We'll discuss that in the next section when we lay out our DocNet plan, to save America's healthcare. For now, we have more cost drivers to reveal that we'll also provide solutions for. In theory though if we remove 48% of the claims including the claim and their associated costs to the insurance company; we should realize a potential 48% reduction in premiums… now, what would that do for your bottom line?

Waning competition of insurance plans

Words like "choice" and "competition" and my favorite "If you want to keep your health insurance plan, you can" were often touted when the Administration conceded to the idea of the Senate version of healthcare reform. All of those things sound great but what happens when insurers, who, by the way, were in on the design of the Senate plan from the beginning, start to drop less profitable plans?

We would have to pay more for a plan in the insurance exchange; that's what. We're already starting to see evidence of this going on now.

Reported by 27 East: Empire Blue Cross Blue Shield, the state's largest health insurer and one of the largest for small businesses, announced to health insurance brokers on Friday that it will eliminate most of its small group plans in the New York market effective April 1, 2012, and is slashing its financial incentives for brokers to sell those products—a move one industry insider has said would be "catastrophic" for the insurance marketplace.

In a statement, Empire, also the biggest insurer on the East End, said it will reduce the number of plans offered to small groups and will offer fewer PPO, HMO and EPO plans, but claimed it has no intention of withdrawing from the market.

Reported by Courant: CIGNA Corp has announced that it will no longer offer small-group health plans through the CBIA. The company's exit coupled with a decision last year by Health Net to stop offering insurance in the Northeast reduces the CBIA's number of health-insurance carriers from four to two. Small businesses will still be able to buy health plans offered by ConnectiCare and Oxford, which is a part of UnitedHealth Group.

Insurers eliminating the available plan options reduce our available choices, which force us into higher premium plans with lower benefit options. And, keep in mind that insurance company lobby groups pressured Senators for this particular healthcare reform. There is no doubt that insurers are as culpable as the politicians in the continued premium crisis we are facing. However, they're hiding behind politicians in order to keep pricing high by shifting the responsibility of creating consumer based products, to politicians passing laws and writing rules. What they fail to see is that they've crawled in bed with the enemy of the free market, and in the end most of them will lose everything as we drift or speed toward more government control.

This newfound cooperation between private industry and government is as dangerous in the health insurance industry as it has been in the housing industries with Fannie Mae and Freddy Mac. This government, private business hybrid has been tried and it's been an unmitigated disaster that Washington still has dealt with. I ask you, has either of these responsible industries for the housing crisis been dealt with? That's the same potential with the health insurance industry and the coupling of a government/private partnership.

Who else is controlling what plans are made available to you and your family? You may be shocked to find out that the state governments also control which plans you can purchase! Every state has a Department of Insurance or similar entity. One of their primary roles is to approve the policy designs presented to them by the insurers. Each policy is scrutinized for what the state feels are necessary provisions and exclusions, as well as, in many states, what the insurer can charge in premiums for each plan. The approval process is often arduous and reduces an insurer's ability to adjust quickly to market changes. Now don't get me wrong here, I'm not advocating for the complete dismantling of the Insurance departments or a complete deregulation of the industry, just a less stringent one, so that insurers can compete and adjust to markets.

Don't take my word for it either. Look up your state's department of insurance and ask what's required for a new insurance company to do business in your state. Inquire what its requirements are for a new policy to be offered within the state.

The next level of control is the employer who chooses which plan will best suit their needs according to what they or their benefit coordinator chooses. Now, if the employer is paying for you to have that coverage as a paid benefit, then that's all well and good and they should have a say in the amount of coverage you receive. My experience is that most employers don't pay for dependent coverage, but because they chose the plan to be offered, they've effectively removed options for you, the employee, to pick the best and most affordable coverage for yours and your family's specific needs.

Many Americans get caught in the desert of limited options when they can't get access to an insurance plan through their work and can't qualify for a government subsidized insurance plan. Many can't afford to add their dependents to their coverage at work because of the high premiums of a group policy and with the limited choices offered it leaves the open market as their only hope for a plan option.

Personally I've found that too many people believe that the open insurance market is more expensive than group insurance and more times than not they're incorrect. However, the point is the same; there are too many people deciding what health insurance choices we should have instead of the free market choosing based on the needs of the consumer. That's doesn't support competition, the way competition was meant to work in free markets.

The bottom line here is that whenever an industry is so heavily controlled, competition can't truly thrive. It's where we see heavy competition that high prices are controlled, and the highest quality and quantity of services are provided. Because price points matter; if you can buy almost the same product or service and you can choose to pay less by picking a different company or provider it is near certain that you'll go with the less expensive one; with the exception of poor customer service, there is no reason to pay more. We're always looking for the best deals, that's what makes black Friday so popular.

Increased doctor patient ratios due to lack of doctors

There is a growing and dangerous health cost crisis which is looming over America today. Its simple mathematics but we're short the doctors needed to tend to the growing population of America. We'll discuss some of the reasons why later but the gist of it was written about by USA Today which reported:

The number of U.S. medical school students going into primary care has dropped 51.8% since 1997, according to the American Academy of Family Physicians (AAFP).

Considering it takes 10 to 11 years to educate a doctor, the drying up of the pipeline is a big concern to health-care experts. The AAFP is predicting a shortage of 40,000 family physicians in 2020, when the demand is expected to spike. The U.S. health care system has about 100,000 family physicians and will need 139,531 in 10 years. The current environment is attracting only half the number needed to meet the demand.

At the heart of the rising demands on primary-care physicians will be the 78 million Baby Boomers born from 1946 to 1964, who begin to turn 65 in 2011 and will require increasing medical care, and the current group of underserved patients.

How does that drive costs up?

Well, it's a simple matter of the economic theory of supply and demand. There are only so many hours in a day and out of each day there are so many working hours available (even doctors need sleep after all).

If the total number of patients who need a doctor exceeds the total number of available doctors with a limited number of working hours, then the demand for available doctors increases. As demand increases the more they will rightfully charge for their time; but it also means they'll have less time to spend with each patient understanding the patient's problems making effective diagnosis more problematic.

The Association of American Medical Colleges (AAMC) suggests that Congress lift the current cap on Medicare funded residencies as a way to address doctor shortages.

"...there is no real substitute for raising the residency cap. Grover said the AAMC is hoping to work with members of Congress and others to expand residency slots by 15 percent, or an additional 4,000 slots per year, which would be phased in to mirror a projected 30 percent increase in medical school enrollment.

Although lawmakers seem more aware of the impending physician shortage, a sluggish economy and the new focus on reduced federal spending will present a challenge to keeping residency cap issues on the congressional radar."

The Georgia Health Sciences University suggests that the shortage is largely caused by the disparity of cost versus reward for going into Primary Care medicine stating:

The nation's shortage of primary care physicians has been linked to a host of poor health outcomes, and a study published in the Journal of the American Medical Association suggests that salary disparities play a major role in the shortage.

We want more doctors, and we want them to be effective while at the same time putting demands on them for perfection. There are currently no good incentives to become a doctor. (We'll address the solution to this problem in the DocNet chapter).

We must have an adequate number of doctors to care for the primary concerns of the population or we will run into problems of which costs will only be one of them. Instead, we are just driving them away:

The assault on the medical profession by the legal profession

Lawyers, at least the ones most often referred to as 'ambulance chasers'; well there's a reason that they are both feared and often hated in America especially by the medical profession because they've have targeted the healthcare industry and suing doctors, hospitals and drug manufacturers as an income strategy for their practices.

There are entire law firms dedicated to medical malpractice; just type the word 'misdiagnosis' into your Google search engine and the tenth result down as of the writing of this book was for the medical malpractice firm of Cirignani, Heller & Harmon.

Their areas of specialty are according to their website: Medical malpractice, birth injury, hospital mistakes, medication errors, misdiagnosis, stroke complications, spinal cord injury, brain injury, paralysis injury, anesthesia injury, nursing home abuse and wrongful death.

Is there a real need for full time attorney to litigate in the areas of each of these declared specialties?

Quite frankly yes, we don't want the medical profession to act irresponsibly and needlessly cause injury or death of anyone. On that point, we can all agree but where is the line of responsible litigation and malicious litigation for the benefit of an attorney payday?

According to Tillinghast, an actuarial practice focused on insurance; who conducted a study of the malpractice system, and their conclusion includes both reasonable and frivolous lawsuits: Their findings according to a WSJ.com article:

The dollar figure comes from an annual estimate of tort costs by the Tillinghast arm of consulting firm Towers Perrin, which in turn is based on insurance data from A.M. Best. Tillinghast adds together the money paid to third parties as a result of tort claims; money spent by insurance companies to investigate and defend claims; and administrative expenses to handle claims. The group said the total cost in 2005, the latest year available, was $260.8 billion; that works out to about $880 per person, or $3,520 for a family of four.

Even if only 10% of these cases were, in fact, "frivolous" that's a $26 Billion expense that will be calculated into the premium costs, which is then passed onto consumers and taxpayers. Of course, it's 2012 the number of medical injury and other claims are certain to have gone up; that means the cost to defend them has gone up too, resulting in the overall cost of medical malpractice insurance being higher, along with all of our premiums.

The higher cost to make or provide a service or for medical device companies to manufacture a product translates into doctors raising fees to cover costs and losses, and that means you and I pay higher premiums to get the coverage we need.

While it may be true that in the grand scheme of things $26 or $30 or even $50 Billion, is an infantile amount in comparison to the total cost of healthcare; it is an expense that we can reduce and should reduce to help drive costs down. We should note, the real cost of these lawsuits isn't in the suits themselves but in the attempt by doctors to preempt a defense.

Defensive medicine

If, as we've just covered, medical malpractice suits are such a meaningless cost in the broader sense, then it does beg the question, why everyone seems to agree that defensive medicine is an out of control cost that must be addressed.

According to the American Academy of Orthopedic Surgeons (AAOS):

In recent studies, more than 90 percent of physicians reported practicing positive defensive medicine in the past 12 months; unnecessary imaging tests accounted for 43 percent of these actions. More than 92 percent of surgeons reported ordering unnecessary tests to protect themselves.

Another study found a direct relationship between higher malpractice awards and malpractice premiums and Medicare spending, especially with imaging services. The increased spending, however, had no measurable effects on mortality.

In a recent Gallup survey, physicians attributed 34 percent of overall healthcare costs to defensive medicine and 21 percent of their practice to be defensive in nature. Specifically, they estimated that 35 percent of diagnostic tests, 29 percent of lab tests, 19 percent of hospitalizations, 14 percent of prescriptions, and 8 percent of surgeries were performed to avoid lawsuits.

With these statistics, it's easy to see why things have skyrocketed out of control. If 34% of all medicine practiced is defensive, the costs to consumers and taxpayers could easily be in the hundreds of billions of dollars per year. Is it any wonder why, no matter what policy or control the government wants to implement, the cost continues upward?

Defensive medicine is costing us all as the medical profession attempts to shield itself from the legal profession, or provide a viable defense for when they find themselves on the wrong end of a lawsuit.

That report also told of the indirect costs of medical malpractice suits on the industry:

Beyond the financial costs, the lack of physician liability reform and the practice of defensive medicine restrict patient access to care from physicians who limit their practices as well as from a decreasing supply of physicians. In one study, 42 percent of responding physicians had restricted their practices to avoid risky procedures, patients with complex conditions, or those perceived to be litigious.

Truthfully, this just illustrates how we've become a protectionist society because too many of our citizens want "what's coming to them" when all that used to be required was honor. Honor used to be the remedy to this type of situation because those of us with honor knew (as the rest of us should know), that doctors are just like us—they're human and they will from time to time make mistakes. Not intentionally, of course, but they do make them. However, if there were any honor in the medical profession, doctors who made a mistake would do what was necessary to make it right.

Lawyers with honor wouldn't view the medical profession as another income stream but would use their influence to ensure that the medical profession did their very best to remain honorable.

Of course, then there's us, within our ranks are those who lack honor and look through the lens of what's fair instead of what's right, and those are the ones being used by the lawyers who only view the medical profession as an income stream.

Again, I'm not saying that doctors shouldn't be held accountable. I would never suggest that; but what I am saying is, if we operated from a position of honor to start with, we wouldn't need to force others to do the right things.

All that medical malpractice lawsuits have done is to create a distrustful environment where CYA is the theme. Doctors feel they need to practice large amounts of defensive medicine because if their diagnosis is called into question any attorney worth the $200 or $300 per hour would strap them to a pole and run them to the top of it, and they'd be out to dry and made to pay.

We recently experienced this when my wife had repeated and unexplained bouts with blood pressure spikes. Granted it was to a point where it caused her to be sick to her stomach and we considered it serious. When we saw the doctor she ran initial tests, did an EKG and then told my wife she also needed to have an echocardiogram and a CT scan and blood tests that ran the length of two sheets of paper.

And why?

Because her blood pressure was high with no other symptoms of heart, or other related care concerns. But that was of no consideration by this doctor because she wanted to be sure of her diagnosis.

I'm all for caution, but it was over the top and almost obvious that this doctor, I believe, through no fault of her own, was being excessive to avoid a potential mistake. My guess is that she's had a legal problem or at a minimum a legal scare in the past, and she wanted to make sure it never happened again.

Needless to say, we received a second opinion and some blood pressure medication; and my wife is doing great, but I can't imagine how much my cost for all those tests would've been, and for our insurance company had we stayed with that doctor. What I do know is that it would have been a considerable amount; I only said no because I understand the result (maybe our insurer should send me a thank you card or something similar).

All joking aside; we literally can't afford to keep this up. We need to come to grips with the facts; doctors do their very best to provide us with the best information and diagnosis they can and if they make a mistake but try to make it right, we should leave it at that; at least that would be the honorable thing to do. Overreacting to fixable mistakes is costing us all and we need to decide as a society, what help someone who's been injured by a medical mistake can get and try to keep the lawyers out of it as much as possible.

Alright enough about that lets move forward.

<u>Burdensome insurance regulations by states governments</u>

It's fairly safe to say that most people aren't aware of the strenuous requirements that an insurer has to go through to create and offer an insurance policy within a resident state. So, let me explain it in its basic form; an insurer MUST get every policy for which they intend to sell to the public approved by each state's insurance department, regardless of whether they are licensed in a particular state; or have done business there for years. And there are 50 states at last count (or was it 57?… sorry, I couldn't resist).

That means that if they want to offer the same plan in every state they simply can't, because each state also has their own minimum requirements of what must be covered and/or what can't be covered. For example in Texas, a very business friendly state, is one of the worst when it comes to approving new insurance policies to be sold by insurers; but even they have "mandated" coverage. Take a look:

Cardiovascular Disease Screening Tests For Early Detection:

Citation: TIC Chapter 1376

Plans that cover medical screenings must provide coverage for up to $200 for computed tomography or ultrasonography screening tests every 5 years. The tests *must be performed by a laboratory that is certified by a national organization recognized by rule.*

Coverage must be provided to males older than 45 years of age and younger than 76 years of age and to females older than 55 years of age and younger than 76 years of age, if the enrollee is diabetic or has a risk of developing coronary heart disease.

However, there have been clear attacks levied against insurers for not providing certain coverage or dropping policyholders in their time of their need.

The Christian Science Monitor reported on such claims from President Obama:

In a speech on Monday, President Obama charged that insurance companies have made a calculation that they can deny coverage for preexisting conditions, drop coverage when people need it most, and make big profits "as long as they can get away with it."

"Since there's so little competition in the insurance industry, they're OK with people being priced out of health insurance because they'll still make more by raising premiums on the customers they have," Mr. Obama said, during remarks at Arcadia University in Glenside, Pa.

This is all very good rhetoric, but it simply isn't reality; what is, are the political and capitalistic forces at odds. An insurance company needs to be profitable to stay in business so there are times when people will be terminated from coverage, but because consumers can report insurers to the state insurance departments and these companies have to answer every charge, it's highly unlikely the termination is without cause, but politicians need to at least appear to care about the people, so many them use insurance companies to political gain.

In the end, the more mandates that are placed on insurers to provide more coverage; the more our premiums for insurance must be in order to pay the claims of those mandated provisions. It really is that simply. And, the more people that are covered through mandates that have pre-existing conditions as will be the case if Obamacare is allowed to stand, the more the cost of healthcare will skyrocket.

You see every insurance company has what we lovingly call "bean counters" who are the actuaries. What these bean counters do is determine how much an insurer will pay out in claims every single year down to the penny and the truth is their process is very accurate, far more accurate than even the famed CBO. They can tell you to the number how many people will have a heart attack this year and how many will likely survive plus how much it'll cost the insurance company. It's all based on actual numbers of people who contract certain illnesses and how much the treatment of those illnesses costs. I won't bore you with the actual process because it's a truly mind numbing experience, and you have to be a mathematician to grasp all the data (you may be but I'm not). Politics, sound bites and the feelings of Americans don't play a role in a actuary's outcome, because it's based purely in numbers.

The more mandates handed down by state insurance departments and Obamacare the more the costs goes up because the numbers of claims being paid will go up, and governments seem to want to mandate inclusion of the sick and needy, which, on the surface seems noble cause but in real terms costs us all; it's that simple.

One other thing to note here is that most state insurance departments also approve every increase in premium requested by an insurer and they must show proof of why they need to increase premiums. Healthcare.gov states on their website that 26 States and the District of Columbia have the authority to reject a proposed increase that is excessive, lacks justification or exceeds certain standards. Of course, they blame the insurance companies for increasing premiums in the states with limited or no premium oversight when it's clear that more than half of the states make that decision for them.

No matter how you look at it mandates cost insurers money and, therefore, cost us in premiums.

One last thought on the subject of mandates on insurers. When pre-existing conditions are mandated, they will have effectively removed personal responsibility of the consumer. The result, many Americans will buy insurance when they have a medical need and drop it as soon as the insurance pays the claim. It's what many people already do with dental insurance and that cost is passed on to all those who keep paying their premiums. What an incentive to be responsible, huh.

Government health programs drive up private healthcare costs

Another issue that's occurring today in the Medicare and Medicaid programs; that is nearly guaranteed to happen somewhere in the future should Obamacare be deemed Constitutional; the price fixing of doctors and hospital fees.

I'm sure you've heard Congress repeatedly refer to a remedy to a Medicare problem they call the "Doc Fix". It's an annual measure taken up by Congress to fix a disparity between to formula used calculate how much Medicare will pay doctors for their services and the annual increase in healthcare costs. So each year, the doctors' face a potential cut in revenues until Congress acts, try and plan your family budget on Congress, how hard would that be?

The debate has been shifting in Washington in recent years over whether or not to even vote on the doc fix, leaving doctors to feel the pinch of continually reduced payments for their services by the government. For example, Sarah Kliff of the Washington Post says that American doctors are paid better than other developed countries and for that we should reconsider fixing the Medicare payments made.

This as well as the growing divide in Congress on how fund and structurally change Medicare in the future; to which many have concluded is causing doctors to rethink how many if any Medicare patients they'll treat.

According to USA Today:

1. The American Academy of Family Physicians says 13% of respondents didn't participate in Medicare last year, up from 8% in 2008 and 6% in 2004.

2. The American Osteopathic Association says 15% of its members don't participate in Medicare and 19% don't accept new Medicare patients. If the cut is not reversed, it says, the numbers will double.

3. The American Medical Association says 17% of more than 9,000 doctors surveyed restrict the number of Medicare patients in their practice. Among primary care physicians, the rate is 31%.

4. The federal health insurance program for seniors paid doctors on average 78% of what private insurers paid in 2008.

"Physicians are saying, 'I can't afford to keep losing money,' " says Lori Heim, president of the family doctors' group.

The underpayment and delayed payment of doctor fees by the government are helping drive up the costs to full paying, insured patients because, as we've stated before, all losses are calculated and then passed on in the form of higher fees. The higher fees aren't passed on to the government to pay either; it's put onto the back of the insured, paying consumer in additional premiums that'll pay the difference. So we must bear the burden of the government's inability to pay their bills to doctors in full, as well as pay our own bills…. sounds fair, right? As the doctors increase their fees to be charged to insurance companies, the premiums are increased to offset the higher doctors' fees and the endless cycle of increase continues.

Let's look at it from a different perspective; imagine you own a little bakery down the street from your house, and you sell your bread for $1.00 per loaf, and your business is largely successful; making you very proud of what you've been able to accomplish. One day, the government implements a program and tells you that they'll pay for the bread for those who can't afford to buy bread (yes, I know it's a ridiculous analogy but go with me here). You agree because you're still going to get your $1.00 per loaf; a dollar is a dollar after all…right?

Then the government realizes, that too many people have jumped onto the free bread program they've created, and they are soon short of funds for the program, to pay you for the bread that you still provide as a condition of your contract with the government. The longer it takes them to pay you, the less operating capital you have to work with, and though it's a struggle you still manage to pull it off, so you keep going because you know that the government will eventually pay you. At least that's what you've always believed.

Then the government realizes that they're in over their heads on this program because even more people have become aware and "qualified" to receive the bread, but it is far too unpopular to raise taxes to cover the difference, of your cost and their revenues and it's certainly too popular a program to cut from the government budget. So, their solution, they come to you and say, "Sorry, but we're no longer able to pay you the full value of the bread you provide under this program. So, from now on we're going to pay you $.75 per loaf; but don't forget that if you don't continue to provide the bread to the people we are helping, everyone is going to see you as a business that hates the elderly and children, so you just keep providing that bread."

Now did your cost to make the loaf of bread go down?

No, but now you have to make up for the $.25 loss on each loaf of government bread that you sell, and, you have no choice but to add the loss from the government to the price of the bread everyone else buys, or you'll just go out of business financially. Now your customers come in and if it's one paying customer to one customer on government assistance, the paying ones would have to pay $1.25 for a loaf of bread instead of $1.00. What happens when the people on government assistance outnumber the paying customers? Let's face it, it's unsustainable by anyone's standards.

This is a massively simplified example of exactly what's happening to doctors when they take on patients with government programs, but it's an identifiable cost driver and it must be dealt with, if we're ever going to solve the health cost crisis in America.

Uncompensated care and free loaders

Uncompensated care is the unpaid obligation for care, based on a hospital's full established rates, for patients who are unable or unwilling to pay their bill. Unlike within a charity care situation, bad debt arises in situations where the patient has either not requested financial assistance or does not qualify for financial assistance. In these cases, the hospital will generate a bill for services provided. For uninsured patients, the amount of bad debt can pertain to all or any portion of the bill that is not paid. For patients with insurance, certain amounts that are the patient's responsibility -- such as deductibles and coinsurance -- are expensed as bad debt if not paid.

Why is Uncompensated Care Important?

It's important because costs incurred by hospitals for providing this care must eventually be paid by someone. Hospitals are forced to shift these costs to other payers both individual and government but typically private insurance companies. This is referred to as the "cost shift".

How Does Uncompensated Care Affect You?

Uncompensated care and inadequate reimbursement by government insurance programs like Medicare and Medicaid, as we just explained, end up affecting everyone because they obviously contribute to the increased cost of health care. Costs incurred treating patients that are not reimbursed end up getting shifted to private insurers and state governments, who only pay a portion. This "cost shift" is a broad contributing factor to why annual increases in healthcare costs are typically greater than general inflation. When hospitals are forced to raise their rates to cover unpaid costs, private insurers must raise their premiums.

Since most private health insurance is paid by employers, business ends up paying the bill, which translates into additional operating costs for non-medical related businesses and that too is passed on to consumers. Plus, as their costs for healthcare rise, businesses are forced to either reduce benefits to employees or require their employees to pay for a greater portion of their monthly premium. Usually, it'll amount to a combination of all these measures.

The state and federal government pays a portion of the expense but leaves the majority to be absorbed. In 2010, the average cost for uncompensated care for the 4985 community hospitals was $39.3 Billion according to the American Hospital Association survey which is conducted each year, and that's just the community hospitals.

In 2005 NewsMax reported:

For 12 states, the government pays hospitals for providing emergency services to illegal aliens. In 2005, the state of California got $70 million to help with dismal shortfalls. California's San Diego County was about $100 million in the red and Los Angeles County about $140 million.

Many California hospitals cannot afford to absorb costs and many are forced to close due to financial mandates for treating illegal immigrants. As recently reported, 84 California hospitals are closing their doors forever.

Since more than 7 years has passed, the problem created by uncompensated care has only increased especially in the years where we've been in recession.

We must also take into consideration the cost of illegal immigration on uncompensated care. Not to stir the hornets' nest over the illegal immigration debate but about 25% of all uncompensated care is directly linked to illegal immigrants who receive care. The Journal for American Physicians and Surgeons completed a study on the issue of illegal immigration and the costs to healthcare. You can review their full report here.

The broader point is that uncompensated care whether from American citizens or illegal immigrants is adding to the bottom line costs of providing healthcare in America, no matter which side of that debate you're on. So, how do we fix it?

I have a plan that'll address each of these issues, drive down costs and make healthcare in America once again affordable for everyone including the government.

Chapter 8

The DocNet Solution to Revolutionize Healthcare Delivery and Its Costs

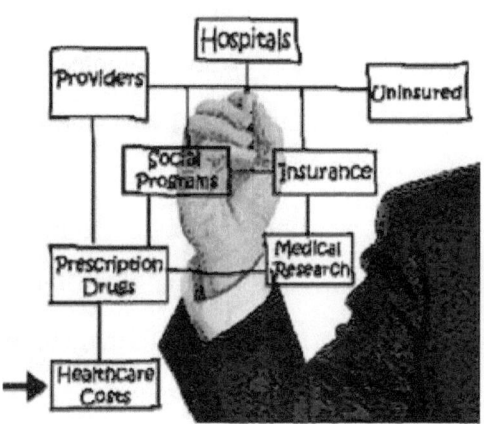

As you can see, we've our work is cut out for us if we hope to have an efficient and cost effective health insurance and care delivery system, which more of our citizens can participate. However, in order to solve the health costs issue in America we just need to take a couple steps back; look at the progression of the insurance industry; take the cost drivers we've identified and eliminate or reform them. In other words, we have to look outside how we see healthcare delivery today for the solution of tomorrow... a free market solution.

There is no better country than America to solve this important and delicate issue. America is the land that has revolutionized the world more than once. Modern medicine is a direct result of the innovation created by entrepreneur's right here; the Band-Aid, the portable dialysis machine and even the disposable diaper were invented in America. Surely, we can find that American pioneering spirit to solve this problem too. And I've developed the blueprint that can transform American health care delivery to meet the needs of every American…and I call it the "DocNet". Now, I'm just one guy, with one idea, so just imagine what could happen if we unleash the American entrepreneurial spirit on this issue. I believe this problem could be solved quite literally overnight.

That being said, this solution, the DocNet is a revolution in the delivery of healthcare in America. It has the potential to resolve the issues we face as individuals and as a nation in the ever rising cost climate of healthcare today. As we've discussed already, we don't have a quality of care issue in America; we have a health cost crisis. So all we need to focus on, is reducing that cost; that's the solution to the problem, and that is what the DocNet will do.

So how can Doc Net revolutionize healthcare delivery?

By returning the insurance companies to the business of insurance, which is the prevention of catastrophic monetary losses during major medical events and acute care; these are things like heart attacks and major accidents. I could give you a list of all the medical terms that would be considered major medical such as 'myocardial infarction' but really, who wants to read that? So we'll leave it to the simple explanation for now of major medical events and accidents. The DocNet would be a direct system where the primary care physician would provide your primary and maintenance healthcare services for a direct monthly fee, as opposed to a fee for service payment system.

Of course, the obvious dilemma is, we've grown so accustomed insurers paying doctors, and we only pay a co-pay. But what if I told you, we would eliminate the need for co-pays altogether? We can, and we can create a system where, when you need to see a doctor, you see one; they treat you, and that's it; you're done; no waiting for the bill in the mail, or the medical collections people to call you with threats. You'd just go and get treated and go home.

I know it sounds crazy, but at one time so was flying, but that seemed to work out. Anyway, that's exactly how it worked during the process that created the first insurance plan? If you've ever heard of Blue Cross Blue Shield, then you've heard of the original hospital and physician care plans. Blue Cross was created for teachers and paid for 21 days in the hospital. While Blue Shield was created for Lumber and Mining companies who put a doctor on retainer with a monthly payment to treat their workers, it wasn't until the 1980's that the two companies merged; but I'm not here to give you an insurance history lesson; we want to solve the problem with health costs, right?

Even so, this very short explanation of its history provides us the clues we need to solve this very tough issue of healthcare delivery today. As it was then, we MUST separate insurance from health services or primary care services. We buy insurance to cover us in the event of a substantial financial loss like getting into a major car accident or having a stroke. That's what insurance is for; it's the same in other types of insurance. Life insurance covers the potential loss of income of an income producing family member, and car insurance pays for car damage in an accident, but we don't buy car insurance to pay the mechanic to change the oil (for now we don't). No, we buy car insurance so that in the event of an accident we aren't stuck spending thousands of dollars to buy another car while still paying the one that was wrecked.

So, why does health insurance pay for doctor visits? Because, at one point, we were made to believe that if we had regular checkups, doctors would be able to detect and treat major illnesses before they escalated into costly treatments. It sounded good in theory, but it proved ineffective in practice.

Insurance evolved from major medical insurance, that did exactly what we are talking about which is protection against catastrophic financial losses cause by a major medical event, to what is referred to as comprehensive health insurance; basically major medical health insurance with the added bells and whistles of doctors, drugs, labs and specialists all included in the coverage.

By reverting back to a major medical coverage and eliminating the practice of a third party payment system of insurance companies paying for health services, would allow costs to stabilize which helps maintain affordability for the average consumer.

That is what the DocNet will do in its simplest explanation. But let's look a bit closer a what it all means to you and me.

Chapter 9

Why The DocNet Will Work For Everyone!

The first and most obvious answer is that it'll save you money in premiums. We all like things to be constant...predicable even. With health insurance, it's far from predicable. At the moment, even when we give our insurance card over to the nurse at the front counter, we aren't 100% guaranteed that our insurance plans cover that visit or if weeks after our appointment, we'll receive a bill in the mail for services not covered by our insurance plan. I don't know about you, but I'd rather know how much it'll cost out of my pocket right up front and be afforded the opportunity to pay up on the spot. If I know ahead of time that the insurer would refuse to pay, depending on the urgency of the reason for my visit, I may think twice about seeing the doctor.

For example, two years ago our third child was born, and in an attempt to be responsible parents, we took her to the Pediatrician. We got her the two week check up; then we took her back at two months as was the schedule for immunization shots all the way up to her 18 month well visit; soon after I received a $100 invoice because the insurance company wouldn't pay for the 18 month visit. Now, we pay nearly $400 per month for our children to be covered on our health insurance, but they don't pay for all of the necessary well visits? Isn't that odd? Not really if you understand why, and now I hope you do; they pay for the visits that the insurance company deems necessary and are within their actuarial tables of being "usual and customary" and not the ones the doctor recommends.

It's this type of uncertainty, coupled with the continual increases in premiums, that are the problem for many of us. The DocNet can eliminate this exact problem, stabilizing the costs and making health services once again predictable, which gives us the ability to budget for all of our medical costs.

What we're talking about is a flat monthly fee paid directly to doctors to provide primary health services; very similarly to the original Blue Shield plans. Our research has indicated the potential for a substantial reduction in the direct costs of health services is very high. Based on my own research and an internal estimation (of course, each doctor will determine the cost and fees charged under this system) it's been determined that the markets in states like Texas could be as little as $50 per month or less per adult for primary care services and would be applicable in other states where the cost of living and medicine are lower. Now the people in places like New York, could expect to pay about three times that, but $150 for New Yorkers for health services is cheap considering. I just read a story about a guy paying $800 a month for a 78 square foot apartment (a closet really; you've got to see this check it out here). It's no wonder they have a reputation for being upset; I'd be upset too!

If you're a parent, I know the first question is about how this will work for your kids, and I completely understand that question. It's just as feasible for a Pediatrician to charge a similar monthly fee as a primary care physician and would still be vastly cheaper than health insurance. For those with multiple children; Pediatricians under the business model that we'll describe, could, in fact, charge a multiple children fee that would be affordable for families in that situation. The broader point is that the doctor can control the fee and structure fees based on any number of factors including a flat multiple patient fee for families.

Any number of possibilities could exist under this plan because it's a free market plan, and competition between clinics and doctors will encourage price and quality of care controls making it better for all of us.

So the very first benefit to the DocNet for consumers (patients) is cost stabilization and predictability. How many more people could afford basic health services if all it cost were $50 per month, per person? This can make health services affordable for nearly all of us once again; but hang on we have a solution for those who can't even afford that.

For low income and people currently receiving government assistance for your care; we've provided a solution within this strategy that'll cover you under the same plan model which will be discussed in a later chapter, but it would distract from the point here, so, please be patient or just jump ahead.

We know with a reasonable level of certainty that, should we continue to rely on health insurers, government officials or politicians to stabilize the costs; we'd simply end up with more of the same cycle of premium increases and no solutions. To stabilize costs, employers and insurers force us to sacrifice benefits and pay more premiums and when government gets involved everything goes off the rails. The DocNet would increase the services available to us and reduce the rate because we've cut out the third party for health services…the insurance companies.

Additionally, the care we need will be strictly determined by our doctors, who now have an incentive to treat us quickly, effectively, and correctly because they aren't receiving money per procedure. Their goal will be to keep us healthy, so we stay out of their office; and the notion that doctors don't care for their patients but just want to bill the insurance companies would quickly disappear. They'd also be held to a higher standard, because they will be beholden to their patients, and today how information is disseminated on social media outlets like Facebook and others; well, let's just say that bad news travels at light speed on the World Wide Web. A bad doctor would quickly be uncovered and expunged from the market, by the market. The way it should be.

Once again the best part is no unpleasant surprises will show up in our mail boxes weeks after our appointment with the doctor. We won't have to concern ourselves with deductibles and co-pays; we call the nurse, tell her what our health issue is; she gives us basic triage over the phone to determine the severity of our situation. If symptoms make it necessary, we'd be instructed, by the Tele-nurse, to come in to see the doctor or physician assistant; on that advice we just go, we get the medical help or counsel that we need to keep ourselves healthy. If the doctor wants labs, it wouldn't be any issue at all, because it'd be included in the monthly fee. Prescriptions can be included as well along with some specialized care. (I break this out in a bit, just keep reading).

Think of it this way; even though it was unheard of at the time, and no one else thought it could be done, a man by the name of Sam Walton created the first department store, which took several types of stores and consolidated them into departments within the same store; this revolutionized how we buy goods. Today, Wal-Mart sells nearly everything anyone could ever need, or want – including fresh foods and medicine. Now imagine that same concept for health services and then it makes more sense; consolidation of services by nature lowers the cost. The graph on the next page illustrates the concept.

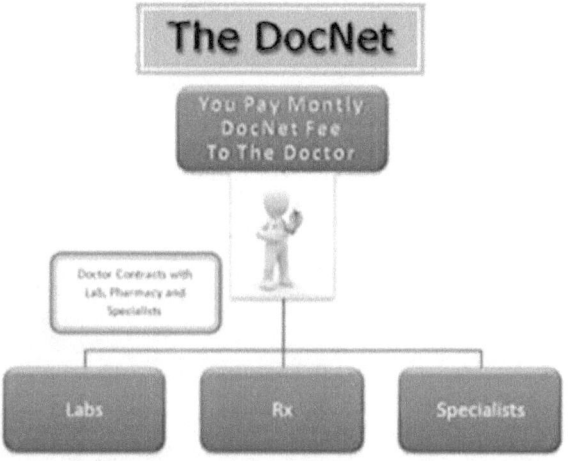

The DocNet consolidates health services so that you pay a specific fee to a doctor you choose, no in or out of network concerns. Your doctor would have secured contracts with the services most used by the patients and included it in the monthly fee. The concept is simple to explain and can also be simple to implement, certainly much easier than reading an insurance contract. It does take some imagination, and a touch of that good old American "can do" Spirit to get to this point, but it can be done.

Now, there are some "experts" out there who think that this is a fantasy and can't be done; but there were people who said that the light bulb would never work either, and I think those are in common use today. Just because it hasn't been thought of by some expert in Washington, doesn't mean that it can't become a reality, besides what does Washington know about creating anything but chaos and complications? That's what's always made America great. The average person could create a solution that meets a market need, and become wealthy or famous in a free market system, but I feel the rabbit hole, pulling me off point, so let me refocus.

Let me demonstrate how the DocNet would work in a practical example: you have a cough, and it's been a couple of days and you haven't been able to shake it. Under the DocNet, you'd pick up the phone and call a Tele-nurse who would listen to you explain, and possibly have you cough to hear, your symptoms, from there they would either make suggestions of a potential self-remedy like rest or a hot cup of tea or over the counter medications that may be effective in your treatment; but if your symptoms sound more problematic, they would schedule you to come to the clinic to be seen by a Physician Assistant. Think about it, for minor things like colds and flu's, not having to leave the comfort of your bed, drive across town to see a doctor, pay a co-pay, to have them tell you that you need rest and drink lots of liquids. That'd be nice!

On the other hand if you had to go in, a Physician Assistant (PA), who is considerably less qualified than a doctor but is qualified in many areas, and is qualified to assist in the treatment and diagnosis of minor illness and injury; sees you and helps determine the next course of action. The PA may be under the direct or indirect supervision of the doctor, but would be a considerable asset to a clinic in providing minor care, amplifying the doctors ability to care for more patients.

The doctor would be the final layer of care you'd have access to when needed. While the majority of patients would be seen by a Physician Assistant who is supervised by the doctor, the doctor's time would be reserved for patients who have more serious problems and require more complicated care.

As an example, let's say you had a cough; you came to the clinic to see the PA; his preliminary screening showed that you had a bit of bronchitis, and just a simple prescription of antibiotic would be all that you needed. The physician assistant would take his diagnosis to the doctor who'd provide a prescription for that medicine and you'd be on your way. On the other hand, if he had reasonable cause to conclude that you potentially had pneumonia he'd get the doctor fully involved in your diagnosis and treatment to ensure your quality of care.

There are distinct advantages to this alternative strategy of care, as it would allow a doctor who has a traditional patient load of 2100 patients to increase that load to 4000 patients, without fear of an overloaded schedule. In basic terms, it maximizes the time of the doctor to be more effective in diagnosis and treatment of larger numbers of patients and not lose quality controls.

This would also be an effective interim strategy to prevent a catastrophe in lack of care with the current doctor shortage. Granted it is a simple solution, but can have major implications, but we don't want to leave it there.

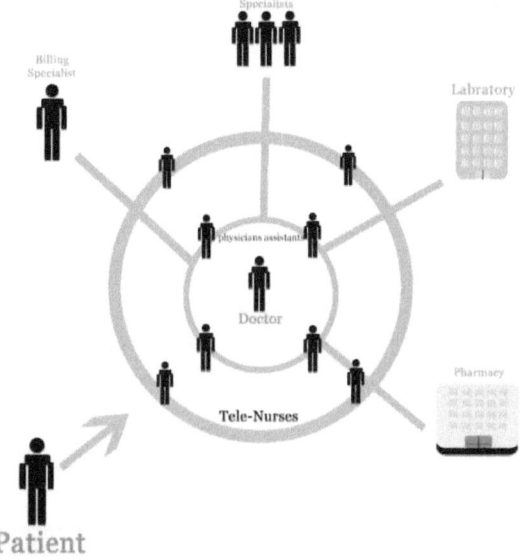

The other component that must be included is an incentive for doctors to transition to this business model instead of remaining with the current one, and we have just the right incentive. Money! This can work, and it can, because in lowering our cost, we increase the amount of money the doctor keeps at the end of the day.

Chapter 10

What's in the DocNet for Doctors

In order for this to work the doctors have to be on board so to speak; not just on board, they have to be motivated to make the change, even in the face of Obamacare. As we've previously discussed we have some issues with a lack of doctors; and without doctors, we have no healthcare, so this is certainly a problem that must be addressed. Remember: It's estimated that, within 15 years, we'll have a shortage of approximately 150,000 doctors according to a Wall Street Journal report. As more and more patients require care, and with fewer doctors to treat them; the old economic standard of supply and demand takes control of pricing. The smaller supply of doctors the more they can and should charge for their services.

The problem we face in America in this area is that we can't mandate people become doctors...that would be called Communism and that certainly isn't the kind of government that Americans want (at least most Americans). So we have two options; we can wait until we're in another "crisis" (a favorite tactic of politicians) and import doctors from other countries, and let the government grabs more control over healthcare. There's only one small problem I can see with that idea, besides government control…how can we guarantee that the doctor coming to treat patients from those other countries are as qualified as those been taught in America? Not to say for certain that they wouldn't be, but really, how can we be sure?

The better option is to provide incentives that would encourage those who would be interested in becoming doctors to take the leap and do it. Nevertheless, it's imperative that we have the right incentives because what's being offered right now, just giving tuition assistance or even free tuition, isn't going to be enough to encourage students to become the doctors we desperately need because they are looking at what's happening in medicine today.

Right now doctors in many states have to be concerned more about making a mistake than treating a patient. They must be knowledgeable or hire people who are, in the fields of insurance claims and government regulations. The burden of cost to start up a practice is on the rise, coupled with the stresses caused by patient loads and underpayments by insurance and government. Not to mention the problems created by ever changing insurance exclusions and the non-payments by patients to add to this perfect storm of disincentive.

The DocNet can solve each of these seemingly impossible problems…Here's how.

First we can create the incentive for new doctors to enter the school and eventually enter the market heading off the estimated shortage in the next one to one and a half decades. The elevator explanation of them is: increase the amount of money that can be made by a doctor's chosen field, while reducing costs to them and their patients; eliminate the need for insurance in the primary care service areas and increase the coverage for major medical services under insurance policies. On the legislative front; reform the qualification and payout structure of Medicare and Medicaid to increase benefits and reduce taxpayer exposure my moving these programs to a premium support model; and lastly reduce the exposure of doctors to lawsuits thereby reducing overhead costs.

Let's take each one at a time and give you the "Well, how would you do that?" explanation.

As we've discussed before, we need to separate care that needs to be insured and care that needs to be directly paid. I might add that this is already on the table with the Republican alternative in the expansion of health savings accounts. Anyway, in order to provide the highest incentive for doctors, to provide maximum care for minimal costs, we need first, to give control of our individual care back to the patient and the quality of that care back to our doctors; in a mutually beneficial relationship.

To achieve that; patients would pay a monthly fee directly to a primary care doctor (PCP) as we discussed before. They, in turn, would build the necessary relationship with other essential providers such as pharmacy, laboratory and specialists and together they'd be able to provide the highest quality of care at the lowest cost to the patient.

Our research has indicated that the proper patient load for a fee for service physician is somewhere between 2100 and 2300 patients depending on who conducted the study. If we were to use this estimate as the basis for the DocNet model, the income side of the physician's ledger would look something like this:

In states like Texas with a monthly fee to patients of $50; we split the difference of the patient load numbers to 2200.

That would produce a monthly income for the doctor's clinic of $110,000 and an annual base of $1.3 million. Keep in mind, this is gross income, and we'll talk about the outgo in a moment. The family practitioner under the current insurance based system makes an average of $160,000 per year, according to the Association of American Medical Colleges (AAMC). I would think that the potential of $1.3 million in gross revenues would be an incentive that will likely bring a flood of primary care physicians into the market; any market for that matter.

With a gross income of $1.3 million, even if the doctor paid out 85% (the same percent insurance companies pay out) of that income, which they wouldn't, but just for arguments sake, if they paid that much out in overhead expenses they'd still increase their take home by roughly $30,000 per year over what they currently make. However, under the DocNet solution the increased overhead is both predictable and manageable which is an advantage to the doctor because they can set the monthly fee that makes sense to their business; not to mention that a doctor's clinic's overhead would be substantially less than that of insurance companies.

However, I contend that because of the efficiencies created by using the DocNet clinical structure, doctors could increase their patient loads to approximately 4000 patients. At that load, a doctor could realize an annual gross of $2.4 million which would give that doctor's office the added benefit of higher capital to work with and provide better care with.

Chapter 11

The Doctors Anticipated Overhead

To help this make more sense we must talk about the expense side of the ledger because the doctor isn't going to pocket $1.3 million. He or she will have their traditional overhead expenses of nurses, possibly some physician assistants and the billing staff; although most physicians will be able to restructure their billing departments due to the simplification processes of the DocNet solution but we'll discuss that further a bit later on.

We've determined that providing the best care under this new approach; that care would be broken down into four parts; primary care, labs, prescription and specialty care. Your primary care physician would be receiving your monthly fee of $50 or more, depending on where you live, to provide the four parts of care that would be needed. However, not all doctors have their own pharmacy; so direct business relationships would need to be established with companies and organizations that doctors feel comfortable in working with.

(We'll stick with a low cost of living area like Texas for this example; because it's what I'm familiar with.)

Medications

Let's begin the breakdown with the largest expense of the four categories, the pharmacy. We all know that many drugs aren't cheap in many cases, and the complexities of paying for drugs under the insurance process are often confusing. You have generic, brand and formulary drugs, and the pharmacy has to tell us which one falls under which category and then we pay the respective co-pay.

This led to a positive turn of events in the open market; large store chains like Wal-mart, local grocery chains, and others are competing with $4 prescription drugs. Commonly used generics are put on a list and offered to the consumer at this discounted rate. It's certain that as time goes on, more of the currently used brand name and formulary drugs will have a generics counterpart and with a more cost effective price tag too; causing the list to continue to grow and then new lists with differing price points will eventually be created. It's reasonable to assume that a $8 list and $10 lists will be created at some point.

Here is just a couple scenarios (because the free market allows for infinite scenarios) of how prescription coverage under the DocNet might look like. Doctor's will establish direct contracts with drug makers and pharmacies to bring the cost of medications down through volume discounting. A doctor or clinic could provide medication at cost directly to patients to increase the value of their clinic (which is an ideal situation) or they may negotiate a discounted rate with a local pharmacy.

Now the one thing that we must keep in mind is that there are no insurance plans that have $0 copay for prescriptions, and typically the copay is between $15 and $60 per prescription depending on the drug type. In this case, your doctor would negotiate specific pricing for the drugs that he or she prescribes directly with a local pharmacy or possibly the drug company itself; in exchange, the doctor would pay that pharmacy or drug company a monthly fee.

Continuing on with this example we've been using of the patient paying the doctor $50 per month; the doctor would pay the pharmacy an $8 per month per patient service fee. A pharmacy that contracted with an office that has a patient load of 4000 patients would collect $32,000 per month in service fees; not including prescription costs agreed to in the contract process. For the 2000 patients that office actually sees and prescribes medications to; the pharmacy would continue a revenue stream from what we now call co-pays, the difference being that instead of the insurance company paying the pharmacy it would become the direct negotiated cost to patients through the doctor's contract. This will work well, especially for generic and even formulary drugs; however, further negotiations directly with drug makers may be necessary for brand named and formulary drugs; otherwise the doctor may prescribe alternatives to keep patient costs down.

The distinct advantage of this is it puts all the decisions of medicinal care between the doctor and the patient because the doctor will be required to help treat a person and help them get the most effective medications the patient requires, but also can afford. Not to mention it will end the less than appropriate method that pharmacies use to increase revenues, by charging the co-pay amount for the insurance instead of the cash price when the cash price is less than the co-pay.

Not long ago I had to take my two year old in because of a cough, and she was prescribed two drugs; an antibiotic, which cost $79, and a steroid, which cost $15, but my insurance copay was $20 for each and I would have been charged $40 for the two medications had I not asked the cash price.

Under this newly formed system; it could very well happen that because of the rise in popularity of generics drugs, and the way the DocNet pays, the pharmacies wouldn't even need to charge the $4 for most drugs. And in that case, when you go to get your medications you'd pay nothing more than you've already paid; your monthly direct payment to your chosen doctor.

The obvious question is why pharmacies would be willing to opt into this system over the current one. As is with most companies the answer is, they'll make more money and reduce their expenditures; as well as eliminate payment delays of insurance companies and government entities.

Here's why.

The doctor's office will have contracted with a pharmacy to receive medications at the discounted price. A monthly fee of $8 per patient will be paid to that pharmacy under the negotiated contract; the fee will be paid every month regardless of which patients are prescribed medications. With one doctor's patient load, (estimated at 4000) a pharmacy could collect as much as $32,000 per month. A pharmacy located in the vicinity of several doctor's offices could capitalize on multiple patients from multiple doctor's offices maximizing their gross receipts. A pharmacy who capitalized on the equivalent of 30 average doctor's offices with 4000 patients could bring in $960,000 per month or $11.5 million dollars a year in gross retail revenues.

Additionally, having such a close relationship with specific doctors would give a pharmacy more manageable inventory control measures, because the doctors predetermine the types and monthly quantity of drugs they most often prescribe. This helps a pharmacy reduce the added expenses of inventorying drugs not commonly used by their DocNet physicians.

SIDE NOTE: This part of the plan focuses on the rise in generics as a viable means of reducing overall costs. Wal-Mart proved that new ideas can flourish with the $4 prescription program, and ever since it's been proven to be a successful program, many other companies have entered into the market with their own versions of the $4 prescription plan. Today you can get $4 prescriptions even at many local grocery store pharmacies. Many of them offer incentives to transfer prescriptions to their pharmacy, which has proven healthy for the free market of pharmacy drugs because competition drives costs down for consumers.

As with all things free market; the $4 prescription is no different. Many sceptics said it could not be done, and yet, today it has been and it's working; which should tell us that the DocNet could be the next idea that, like Wal-Mart's prescription plan, will revolutionize healthcare delivery costs in America for the sustainable future.

As it stands right now, and taking from Wal-Mart's example...not all drugs will immediately be available under this plan, and we'll experience a transition period; but just as we've seen with the $4 prescription; as time goes on and pharmacies become more accustom to this new payment model; more and more medications will be added.

For those who have to have brand name drugs...you'd pay the difference in the costs of the qualified generic and the brand name drug based on the negotiated price that your doctor has obtained through contracting. For those that absolutely have to have, by choice or otherwise, the higher priced drugs, but don't have the ability to pay for those drugs is where honest charities have the ability to be effective. We'll discuss how medical charities play a role in this solution, in a later chapter. The ultimate idea here is to gain access to health services and increase the quality of care and do it in the most cost effective way possible. But with that, comes some responsibility on our part. For those who insist on higher costs drugs, simply be willing to take responsibility and pay for them; or find someone who'll pay for them on your behalf.

For those who insist that there aren't any generic versions of their drug are 99.9999999% wrong. With the exception of newly discovered medical problems, there are almost always other drugs; they may not be the newest but effective all the same. Just ask any Veteran who gets treatment and any of our fine government hospitals and clinics who are using yesterday's advances to treat today's illnesses. And if it's good enough for our Veterans it can be good enough for those who can't pay their own way. We aren't denying you treatment; we are just saying that you have to live within your own means or find the means. Besides, most newly approved drugs in just ten years will be targeted by lawyers for adverse side effects, because of what the drug companies didn't discover in clinical trials, so you might just be better off.

Plus asking society to pay your named brand or formulary drugs if alternatives exist, is like saying that you have to have the brand new car whenever it comes out because yours get 2 miles less per gallon, and we should all pay the difference for you… I don't think so… how about driving the car you have until the price of the new car comes down to where you can afford to pay for it yourself? That's makes it better for everyone.

Besides in our estimation you won't have to wait too long before market forces push drug companies into the way that WE are willing to pay for drugs and not how they want to price them. If you didn't know, they charge more for medication in the United States and they lower the cost, sometimes dramatically, of the same drug they sell to "less economically advantaged" countries…say like Mexico and oddly Canada…but who thought the Canadians had such an economic disadvantage to us? Isn't it odd how Congress won't pass a law making it legal for us to buy drugs from across the border? Can anyone say big giant drug company lobby groups with deep election pockets? I know I can.

The truth is that the drug manufacturers charge Americans far more for drugs because they can, and we pay whatever they ask and think little of it; even though it too drives up costs and impacts our premiums; all while other countries get price advantages even though they have economies that can sustain prices more closely resembling ours…. Yeah Canada, we're on to you.

But this is about potential solutions…. Sorry, I had a brief lapse in positivity.

The DocNet provides a way to include the vast majority of medications Americans consume, and basically in the same way. The only real difference under The DocNet would be who the contract would be between, your doctor and the pharmacy instead of the insurance company and the pharmacy. We'd all benefit by the dramatic reduction in the cost of health insurance and health services making the system function more effectively; driving prices and premiums down.

Labs

Another key component to our care and a way to cut costs in healthcare is laboratory tests. These of course help doctors in determining what health problems you may be faced with so they can properly diagnose and treat you. And it can be included in the DocNet solution.

There are already many doctors' clinic which have laboratories on site, to cut costs and increase profitability. On top of that, with the radical increase in the profitability of the primary care physician under the DocNet payment structure; many more clinics could afford to set up their own labs and possibly even their own pharmacies. It's completely conceivable to see clinics in the very near future be departmentalized, providing the most complete care possible.

However for those that don't set up their own labs and while a transition occurs in strategies; a clinic using the $50 per month DocNet solution, we've designated for the purposes of this example, $4 per participant, per month to be paid to a lab of the doctor's choosing, so they can achieve the best possible volume pricing. For a doctor's office with the 4000 patient load, a laboratory can contract with that office for the service fee which in this example would be $16,000 per month per patient or $192,000 per year.

A laboratory that contracts with 30 offices would receive $480,000 per month in service fees or $5.76 million per year. In the beginning, we'll again see that many laboratory tests will potentially come with some additional co-pays as the market transitions to the monthly service fee model of cost containment in The DocNet but over time the co-pays will be minimized and most will be eliminated all together.

As new technologies and innovations occur in the free market and new tests are developed to determine causation of disease and treatment options, costs will be driven down. Laboratories then can operate on fixed revenues and can more easily budget for the expense of new tests and procedures that help them remain competitive. Those labs that stay with archaic technologies will be phase out by market forces, and they should be. This strategy reinstates the doctor patient controls over individual health and its costs. And that is something I think we can all agree is the desired outcome.

Specialists

Specialists for high probable illnesses can also be included in The DocNet depending on the factors of patient data collected by our chosen physician. In our sample plan, we've included cardiac maintenance care and cancer detection and prevention services. Doctors can contract with regional specialists, to provide early detection and prevention care for the two most common killers in America at a rate of $2 per month per patient for each cause.

The doctor's would pay that fee on their total patient load, no matter the age or health status, so realistically a specialist or clinic could receive a substantial monthly service fee for all potential patients in that area. Of course, it can easily be determined how many actual patients will be seen by a given doctor or clinic in these fields; because mortality and morbidity tables already exist. Insurance companies currently use these to determine cost outlays for each disease which are used to determine the premiums you and I are made to pay. All that would be needed is access to that same data.

Ultimately for the specialists they'd be collecting an income on all potential patients rather than just the ones who require care. In other words, let's take a small town of 15,000 people. A specialist, who may not like the big city life, could set up a modest clinic in that town and collect on nearly every citizen. At $2.00 per participating patient, per month, at only a two-thirds participation rate, that specialist would make $20,000 per month or $240,000 per year. The DocNet actually encourages doctors to seek out smaller communities and creates the monetary incentives for them to do so. This benefits everyone in the long run.

The bottom line is that primary care doctors becomes the principal source of our care, and they determine what the primary needs of all their patients are; then they obtain the services that their patients need and that they want to provide. And as consumers, we can shop for the doctor who include the services that we want to receive, just like we do now when we see the eye doctor.

The next evolution of this standard of care is a clinic structure with multiple doctors who share the costs and benefits of The DocNet which serves only to multiply the amount and quality of care that can be provided.

The checks and balance of this system is the free market, where patients decide for themselves which doctor and included providers deserve their hard earned dollars, to provide their care and customer service that they want and need. I can tell you that if patients aren't happy with a particular service or person in their doctor's office or clinic; patients have the ability to share their experiences with their doctor's office and be taken seriously. Doctors' or practices that fail to take patient's concerns into account, will face the wrath of their patients and quickly be expunged from the free market.

Let me leave you with this, as the last thought. As we've shared with you, a doctors' clinic with the increased patient load that The DocNet strategy allows for, of 4000 patients, would make it possible to increase gross operating capital to $2.4 million, with a business expense load of just over $800,000 (not including taxes). This leaves the clinic with a

$1.6 million budget that could (and should) be used to modernize and improve accessibility to additional health services of that clinics patients. A doctors' clinic with this kind of revenue stream could add a lab if they don't have one; start their own pharmacy to maintain the quality of service provided to their patients, all with the benefit of cost containment. At that level of revenue, you could staff additional specialists and even provide cutting edge medicines.

By eliminating the income disparity for the primary care physician, you encourage entrance into that field, create competition, in which, the best doctors that provide the most comprehensive overall care will survive, at the same time, we reduce the costs to consumers across the board. It's a real win-win for everyone.

Chapter 12

The Major Medical Insurance Component

There is a place even in this system for health insurance but only for the major medical such as accidents that require emergency treatment and major medical events, such as, things that would require hospitalization for like a heart attack or major and long term treatments like cancer.

I went to ehealthinsurance.com and ran a 40 year old male who lives in Texas; I looked for a $10,000 deductible with no doctor visit or prescription coverage and the lowest premium would be $98.24 but a 20 year old male for the same plan was $56.35 which isn't costly at all. Keep in mind that these premiums include the current claims experience and expenses of this particular area. However, when we start to eliminate the small claims for doctor visits, labs and prescriptions it is easy to imagine as a result, that premiums will radically decline (provided that insurers are honest; and regulators regulate properly).

With that information, and the expectation that premiums will come down as claims experience declines; our rough calculations are that a flat fee of as little as $50 per month per person up to $400 per month per person depending on the patient's location. Consequently an indemnity health plan in New York, NY is $181 per month; a HMO is roughly $300 while a PPO health insurance plan is nearly $800 per month! On the other hand, in Texas it's as little as $100 per month (based on a 40 year old male).

If an insurance plan is offered that provides only major medical coverage without covering the health services that would be covered under The DocNet. It would satisfy the health insurers' needs to remain profitable, because of the major reduction in the number of claims and the costs associated with processing those claims, while at the same time, it provides coverage to us for major medical events such as we've already described with no need for co-pays or deductibles and at an significantly reduced premium.

Why only a rough calculation? This is principally due to the fact that actuaries compile massive amounts of data and have formulas that are used to determine premiums; included in that data are mortality and morbidity rates, claims experience and the average charged by doctors for each procedure in a given zip code. In other words, I'd have to become a bean counter in order to provide that information concisely; I'm sorry, but I haven't the time nor the inclination to do so, for every zip code in America.

Actuaries are very special people who are gifted in the area of mundane data and formulas of which appeals to them but not me; I need more excitement than that.

Where does the typical health insurance dollar go?

Nevertheless, this isn't just a random estimate because Blue Cost Blue Shield published a study on how medical dollars are broken down and what they're spent on. And as you can see in the figure above; 33% of every dollar is for physicians services, and of that, I've assumed that 50% of those costs are for physicians for in hospital services along with the 20% of that cost being the hospital services for a total of 37% of the premium cost, for events which result in hospitalization. Add to that, an additional 10% premium for long term treatment (I'm overestimating the total cost to ensure I don't miss anything) for a total medical cost of 47% of what is currently spent for all health services which are related to in some way, major medical and hospitalization events.

That leaves 53% of our premium being spent on other than major medical events which could be included in The DocNet solution instead of funneled through our insurance company in the form of premiums.

So imagine paying 50% to 70% less than what we're currently paying for health insurance coverage, plus the flat fee for health services! As a real world example: to add me to my wife's group health plan right now (and she has a very good plan), it would cost us an additional $463.31 per month. If I were to purchase a major medical insurance plan, added that to a DocNet doctor, my monthly costs could drop to as little as $150 per month. Plus, I would have better benefits and lower out of pocket costs at the point of service.

That illustrates the difference between the strategies, but what you can see developing is a cost effective way to provide total healthcare access for everyone. Some may choose to just by the major medical insurance coverage for the just in case, while others may prefer the access to a primary care physician and nothing else. It would be an individual choice and the individual's responsibility to make sure they're covered, not the premium payer or taxpayer.

Now I believe strongly that it'll cost even less over time, because the claims experience will significantly drop as more and more healthcare costs are shifted from an insurance based payment system to the service base system of The DocNet. Anyone in the insurance industry knows, that aside from the cost of doing business, the smaller the claims experience, the cheaper the premium for that insurance will become. That's the primary reason we see such disparity in the cost of health services and insurance premiums, because it's based solely on location and that area's claims experience.

The DocNet solution could be implemented for hospitals as well in areas where a population could support it. The patients would decide what hospital they'd prefer to be treated in, for events that result in hospitalization; they'd pay a monthly fee to that hospital in advance of care, to provide the care they need, when they need it, eliminating all concerns of cost on the back end of that care. Although this poses a larger challenge to implement, over time it could adequately cover the majority of Americans. The biggest challenge for this potential solution would be, arranging for an exchange of care if treatment is needed outside the chosen hospital. Though this is worth mentioning as a possibility, at this point it isn't a suggested solution to the current challenge we're facing.

However, this may allow patients to carry a catastrophic health insurance plan in place of a major medical plan; coupled with a monthly payment plan to a chosen hospital and a primary care physician under The DocNet, further reducing the out of pocket premium paid by patients.

Now these are ideas that could dramatically help the paying population afford their healthcare coverage, which would bring more consumers back into the market. The prime candidates to draw back in as paying consumers are those who, at one time, could afford coverage but were pushed out of their plans because of skyrocketing premiums.

And now you may be asking what about (fill in your favorite group, who can't afford even this solution).

Well, since I want to present a potential system that can incorporate coverage for all Americans, which is the goal even of the President (or so he says). I've also developed strategies to answer most of the whatabouts too. Yes, I said whatabouts, on purpose; which simply means what about this or that.

So, let's start with the poor.

Chapter 13

Faith Based and Charity Medicine

The answers to providing care for the poor lay exactly where it started, the faith community and charitable organizations. You see, solutions to providing healthcare can reside outside the box, having never resided there to begin with. This is the United States of America, the richest, most giving nation the world has ever known. It was with the blood of American soldiers that two World Wars were fought and won, that delivers Aids medication to the hurting people of Africa. We are the world's first responders to every disaster, every conflict and every need.

In the earthquake and tsunami of Japan, Americans gave even in the midst of the current recession. Remember Haiti? America rallied around this nation and provided billions of dollars in relief. Most other countries would consider Haiti insignificant but not America. The Indonesia earthquake and tsunami triggered the same response from America and her citizens. It seems that wherever in the world we find undo suffering where we can have an impact, we give, we volunteer, and we allow our government in our names to act in a charitable way.

If it's true that we are the most giving nation in the world and are willing to send our doctor's, money, drugs and volunteers oversees to help, why can't we do the same for Americans? Most people, for one reason or another, believe that we don't currently have charities that provide care for people without means. But that tradition in America still exists and must be continued and expanded for the needs of today.

We have hospitals, medical centers, cancer centers and clinics that operate solely on donations. No government intervention, no dealing with insurance companies and rules. Patients come; they see the doctors, are treated and sent home never to see a bill, because the donors have already covered the costs of their treatment.

St. Jude's Children's Research Hospital is just that, a place for families to bring their children with a whole host of diseases to be treated. What's interesting about St. Jude's is that they have a nearly $700 million annual budget which is completely funded by donations. Just read their mission statement.

Mission

The mission of St. Jude Children's Research Hospital is to advance cures, and means of prevention, for pediatric catastrophic diseases through research and treatment. Consistent with the vision of our founder Danny Thomas, **no child is denied treatment based on race, religion or a family's ability to pay.** (emphasis added).

The Mayo clinic, St. Vincent and the Sisters of Charity are some of the other outstanding organizations that serve the public through charitable donations and research grants. I couldn't possibly list them all, but these are some examples of what we could do to help the poor right here at home.

There are also charities that pay for families housing expenses like the Ronald McDonald House, which helps families stay together during a child's treatment at a facility like St. Jude. You eat at McDonald's and drop some change in the box that's in front of the cashier or at the drive up window, but it covers the housing expenses of families, so they can stay close to their child, their doctors and to be present during the various treatments. Cost to the families = $0.

As I said in the beginning of this chapter, this is America, the most generous nation in the world. I know that we can put, the giving and the can-do spirits of being an American together, and provide for our own citizens. We can use these two uniquely American ideals of hard work and innovation to create the solutions of the future for the delivery of healthcare and charity care, and make them work together to create a total solution for everyone. Healthcare for the poor or elderly should never be a political issue, but rather a social and economic issue, that we can all rally around and allow our faith based and charitable organizations, to be the caregivers of those who need our help.

What would happen if we could take the idea of charity hospitals and modify it to conform to medical care clinics that operated through donations? Their mission would be to provide reasonable care to those who can't otherwise pay for their own care. Or maybe doctors could provide a percentage of their time and clinical resources (after all we are showing them how to make infinitely more money here), to providing care for those currently on Medicaid without filing a claim with the state or expecting a payment from taxpayers. Add to that an additional portion of their time and resources to treat Medicare patients. And what the free market, through charitable doctors, will do is eliminate the need for government involvement of anyone's healthcare needs. Wouldn't that be nice?

In this scenario, the only government involvement would be to allow the time given by doctors' to charity patients as a deductible business expense for that doctor or hospital, if we keep the current tax system.

The result could be, we could wipe out the need for government social programs that "help" the poor and the elderly, in a very short timeframe, because they'll already be taken care of. And we can do it the way we do everything in the world, when and where we find a need, giving out of the generosity of our hearts and our free will, for no other purpose than for the betterment of our society. I know it sounds a bit idealistic but, I ask you, has that ever stopped us before? Wasn't it idealistic when Wright brothers were attempting to be the first to give man the ability to fly? Or when Thomas Edison created the light bulb? The very creation of our country was done by men who were idealistic in their belief in freedom and the destiny of America! Idealism is who we are!

It should never be the duty of the government to care for the poor in any society, because it leads to an illness called entitlementitis. The tendency of government is to create dependency, while the tendency of charity is to lift people up, till they can stand on their own. Not to mention that for the faith community; the Bible tells us that it's the responsibility of every believer through our charity, to care for the least among us and quite frankly as a faith community we could be doing more, much more. On top of that, we are called to do it.

Mathew 25: 35 For I was hungry and you gave Me food, I was thirsty and you gave Me something to drink, I was a stranger and you brought Me together with yourselves and welcomed and entertained and lodged Me, 36 I was naked and you clothed Me, **I was sick and you visited Me with help and ministering care,** *I was in prison and you came to see Me. 37 Then the just and upright will answer Him, Lord, when did we see You hungry and gave You food, or thirsty and gave You something to drink? 38 And when did we see You a stranger and welcomed and entertained You, or naked and clothed You? 39 And when did we see You sick or in prison and came to visit You? 40 And the King will reply to them, Truly I tell you, in so far as you did it for one of the least [in the estimation of men] of these My brethren, you did it for Me.*

I can't speak for other faiths, but I believe that most religions have similar calls to help the less fortunate.

No nation in the world is better at encouraging doctors and drug companies to go to third world places to help provide care for the sick and needy. You have organizations like US Doctors for Africa or AMREF who send doctors and supplies to places like Africa. Mega churches and ministers often call congregants to give donations to help minister to places like India and Haiti.

When there's a natural disaster, churches rally to help rebuild communities. This was demonstrated after New Orleans Louisiana was ravished by Hurricane Katrina, or when Joplin, Missouri was destroyed by tornados, and now we'll rally again to help rebuild for those devastated by the tornados in Indiana.

I believe the faith community is missing a first class opportunity to touch the lives of so many Americans, and others, who reside within our borders that are challenged by medical issues but remain without the means to pay. Churches could work to provide for the needs of their own congregations, paying medical expenses of their parishioners, or for the doctors within their congregations volunteer to give basic care to their members. If not churches, then local communities could create their own community medical clinics to provide for the needs of the impoverished within their communities.

Heck, churches or other groups could provide funds to help pay for the monthly fee of a doctor under The DocNet solution that we've just explained, and possibly help to cover the cost of a major medical plan for a period of time for the needy. I would never advocate for an unlimited assistance program because it would draw people with an entitlement attitude, but I leave that to those who'd create these charities.

The major point is that churches, faith groups and charitable organizations should be the caregivers for the needy and the poor. Let's face it, they would be far better custodians of the monies they receive, to help the poor, needy and even the elderly, in donations than the government ever could be with the money the forcibly take from us in taxes, even if politicians wanted to be better with our money. They would also be much more suited to adjust care based on the immediate needs of the people they care for, versus a bureaucratic system of bickering over what and how much to pay for the services of those who need help.

But where there is a will there is not just a way, but an American way, and we can make this work if we develop the will to do it. I'm one of these crazy people who actually believe in the idea of America, its dream and its people. But don't hold that against me.

Chapter 14

Saving The Government From Government Entitlements

This one is a very difficult topic for me because I'm largely opposed to government intervention especially in the area of healthcare. However, I recognize that this system exists and currently helps many people get care that they'd otherwise not get. With that said, the best way to save government programs for healthcare is to get people off them.

How do we do that?

Outside of strengthening and growing the economy, which is a whole other book for another day, we need to lower the cost of care -- dramatically. One idea, is to get governments (both state and federal) off the fee for service payment structure, and allow them to pay the monthly DocNet fee of a Primary Care Physician for those on government assistance. Plus, they could cover some or all of the premium costs for a major medical plan, for those who need help paying their premiums, but only for those who truly need help, and they should have a scale of premium support that is based on what those folks can afford to contribute on their own.

But really, I refer you back to my previous point of the Faith community and charities for Medicaid recipients in particularly. If the government would work with these organizations, allowing them to take the lead in creating programs and alternatives for the elderly and poor, getting government out of the way, it's already been proven by current charitable organizations, that the needs of those Americans will be met, although it may be surprising to some. Better, the need for government intervention and its programs will dissipate.

The same can be said about the elderly on Medicare; a strong charitable solution can take the weight of the enormity of the challenge and get it off the backs of taxpayers and help to strengthen the economy. However, transitioning Medicare recipients would be vastly more challenging because of the ideological divide we face, not because we couldn't meet the challenge. But as an interim alternative solution, allow me to present another logical idea that will help in the transition, and save money for the U.S. taxpayer.

This is according to CNN Money:

With fewer Americans receiving health care coverage through their employers, government-funded programs like Medicare, Medicaid, military health care, the Children's Health Care Program (CHIPS) and coverage offered by various states have had to pick up the slack.

In 2010, 31% of Americans relied on the government for health insurance, up from 24.2% in 1999.

According to the Centers for Medicare and Medicaid Services -- cms.gov:

U.S. health care spending accelerated slightly in 2010, increasing 3.9 percent compared to growth of 3.8 percent in 2009. Total health expenditures reached $2.6 trillion, which translates to $8,402 per person or 17.9 percent of the nation's Gross Domestic Product, the same share as in 2009. (Read the report here)

Medicare and Medicaid expenditures are roughly 23% of the federal budget or approximately $835 Billion dollars. And that's just the programs under the federal Medicare and Medicaid expenditure which doesn't include the amounts that the states contribute to the Medicaid programs. The federal government only picks up roughly 60% of the total Medicaid tab, and leaves 40% to the states (it may vary from state to state). The total federal, state and local government expenditures for healthcare is, $1.072 Trillion!

Source:

http://www.usgovernmentspending.com/year_spending_20 11USbt_13bs1s_1017

Basically, what the government and insurers have always attempted to make us believe is, that the problem of covering the elderly and the poor is just too big. And that the government is the only solution to providing care for these groups.

That's factually inaccurate; in fact if we took the broader number as reported by CNN Money of 31% of Americans being assisted by the government, for their healthcare needs, we come to a total number of 97,076,028 Americans. Based on the Census Bureau statistics total population of 313,148,479, which can be found at: http://www.census.gov/ or by doing a simple Google search.

Let's do this by the numbers:

313,148,479 X .31 (31%) = 97,076,028

So 97,076,028 are on some sort of assistance from the government for their healthcare. Without any charity involvement and only using The DocNet system to approach this; if we were to use an average expense across the country of $125 per month per participant for primary care the total cost to both the federal and state governments would be:

97,076,028 X $125 = $145,614,042,000 ($145.6 Billion)

We already have insurers who've been willing to take on the elderly through the Medicare Advantage plans with little or no cost to the Medicare recipient. Common sense would then tell us, if needed, Medicare recipients would be willing to participate in these plans if they understood that they'd have no loss of benefit, but actually lowered their out of pocket expenses by doing so.

With that in mind, if we were to estimate an average expense of $450 per month, per participant, to enroll in these plans, either Medicare Advantage or an equivalent insurance plans, just for those of us who need premium support and it was funded by taxpayers for the interim.

97,076,028 X $450 per month X 12 months = $524,210,551,200 ($524.2 Billion)

Now when we combine the two costs of the DocNet system and the Major Medical Insurance we arrive at a total national expenditure of:

$524,210,551,200 + $145,614,042,000 = $669,824,593,200 ($669.8 Billion)

$670 Billion is what we've determined, the entire US federal spending on healthcare could be, and that's just the beginning. This is based on the total number of people insured by different government programs as indicated again by CNN Money. Incidentally this includes Veterans as well (which as a nation we owe them their medical coverage and should be proud as a people to pay for it, just as it's been since the Civil War).

I'll back off my soap box now, but here's the deal, as time goes on, and more efficiencies within the system are discovered, the cost curve will change from and upward to a downward trajectory. Truthfully, I believe that the estimates we displayed here are high, but I wanted to leave room for the unexpected, (something unheard of in Washington) and make it more plausible for the "person who believes that the only solution, is a government one" to come around to this authentic, free market solution.

Back to the point, taxpayers are spending *$1.072 Trillion* as a nation, on healthcare expenses and being told that the government is the only way that these folks can be covered, and we just need to suck it up, open our wallets, and allow Uncle Sam to take more and more. Conversely, we've just shown, by the numbers, that it can be different, very different. In this case, it's the inefficiencies of government that are, and continue to be, the problem.

Just moving the money from a fee for service program, to a premium and program support model, we've demonstrated a potential savings of over $400 Billion in just healthcare expenditures of taxpayers. If that's not worth taking a look at, I don't know what would be, because right now it seems apparent that they just want to spend, and keep spending.

Nevertheless, the need for government assistance programs will continue to exist, until we can implement the full dynamic of this solution. That's because it'll take a strong public will, and an entrepreneurial spirit to create the charities, change the insurance plans, and set up The DocNet payment structure, before we can fully transition the poor and elderly from government plans to this type of free market solution.

We also need active participation of the government to support these ideas to make them viable alternatives. Unfortunately, if what we've seen in recent years is an indicator, political lines have deepened and discourse has become vitriolic in nature. So it'll certainly be a steep, uphill battle to reach the tipping point for this solution where the government is concerned.

But maybe we don't have to wait on the government to jump on board. Through the free market, doctors' could take the lead and make a monthly billing option available to the public now. Charities could be created now and as a community we could start to fund and encourage participation by those in need. Maybe, we create the solution and let the government catch up. It could happen!

Chapter 15

Preparing For The Next Generation Of Doctors and Insurance Plans

We have a lack of doctors and that lack is increasing as we've mentioned before.

The Solution: Increase the supply side of healthcare, which are the doctors. As we've discussed, we need more doctors to provide the quantity and quality of the healthcare we want and deserve. We need to create incentives for doctors to fill areas where there are projected shortages.

What incentives?

Just some of the ideas I've been able to come up with: We could increase the number of grants for education to individuals who would be willing to pursue a career in a particular medical field. The grants would include a provision that students would agree to, in which, after successfully establishing a clinic, ten percent of their patients will be charity patients to help reduce dependency on government programs for healthcare.

We could allow new doctors, who create new clinics, in areas and fields where doctors are needed, a five year federal tax waiver to allow them to get their practices off the ground and afford them the chance to succeed.

Of course, we've already addressed increasing the reward for becoming a Primary Care Physician in The DocNet explanation, which would dramatically increase the income potential of doctors.

The facts are; if we need more doctors we find ways to encourage people who would be interested in that field to enter, by creating the conditions that will lead to them making the decision to jump in, which leads us to the next point.

At one point, doctors had the luxury of prestige which was nearly as important as the potential monetary reward for becoming a doctor. We've seen in recent years through the legal and political profession,s both of these incentives being slowly eroded. Income and prestige were valid reasons for students to elect the medical profession, and now it's one to be avoided.

The Solution: Go the way of Texas. Texans for Lawsuit Reforms wrote the following article demonstrating the problem and the result of passing Tort Reform writing:

Prior to 2003, the State of Texas was in a medical crisis.

Doctors were being sued at record pace and for record sums as there was no cap on non-economic damage awards. This caused malpractice rates to rise significantly. One out of four doctors had a claim filed against them each year. Even though 85 percent of those malpractice claims failed to reach trial, they still cost an average of $50,000 to defend. And for those that did reach trial, the cost was about $1.4 million.

In June of 2003 Texas passed a number of comprehensive medical liability reform laws, that have had a major positive impact for Texans.

Some 24,583 new physicians have been licensed in Texas. The Texas Medical Board (TMB) has received 83 percent more applications and licensed 60 percent more doctors in the past four years than in the four years preceding reform. Today, Texas has more physicians per capita than ever before.

Texas is also seeing doctors return to previously underserved areas. The number of obstetricians practicing in rural Texas has grown by 27 percent. Twenty-two rural Texas counties have added at least one obstetrician since 2003, including 10 counties that previously had none. Post-reform, Texas has licensed 212 orthopedic surgeons, representing a 15 percent increase in the number of Texas orthopedists in the past six years.

The American Academy of Orthopaedic Surgeons wrote about the impact of the Texas tort reforms:

In Texas, for example, rates for malpractice insurance have dropped every year since the passage of liability reform, and the number of obstetricians has increased by 192, compared to a net loss of 14 in the 3 years prior to reform.

Texas has also seen an increase in the number of orthopaedic surgeons (up by 162 surgeons). This increase is due to more physicians being willing to start practices in these states, as well as fewer physicians retiring early due to excessive malpractice insurance costs.

Add to that in the latest session of the Texas Legislature they passed "loser pay" laws which will be another deterrent of frivolous lawsuits, and give doctors in Texas, even more leverage to practice good medicine instead of defensive medicine. If we're serious as a people, that it's necessary to drive health costs down, then limits on payday lawsuits are a must.

Why? Because these limits encourage a thriving healthcare market, which helps to improve care and drive down the costs to patients, and these laws need to be implemented across America.

The Wall Street Journal reported soon after tort reform was enacted in Texas, that doctors were flocking to the Lone Star State. The benefits were nearly immediate, as they point out, the sheer number of lawsuits dramatically declined over the course of one year.

Malpractice suits have plummeted. In 2003, before the caps took effect, there were 1,108 medical liability suits filed in Dallas County, the Morning News reported. Only 142 cases were filed in 2004. Last year there were 184.

Proponents of malpractice reform point to Texas as a model. The surge of doctors has helped relieved shortages in some rural parts of the state.

The benefits of these measures are clear; doctors are more willing to practice medicine in states that protect them from abuses of the legal profession, which increases competition within their profession. This helps drive costs down, as doctors try to maintain a certain number of treatable patients within their practices.

After researching the issue in detail for this book and hearing all sides of the debate over tort reform, I've arrived at a conclusion; we need both a mechanism for people to air their grievances against and about doctors' performance or lack of it, and an environment that promotes good doctors to practice medicine freely and honestly, without fear of some dishonest people using them as a way to line their pockets. It must be a balanced approach to this very complex problem, but what we do know is that tort reform in Texas has had the desired effect.

For the opponents of tort reform who swear that this will have no impact on costs I ask only one question: where's your proof? You can't say that the practice of defensive medicine plus increased liability insurance costs and excessive, punitive awards hasn't driven up the cost of doing business in the medical profession. What is provable is, when cost is added to any business; prices go up to cover the additional cost. It takes only common sense to come to that conclusion, not to mention the ample proof in other industries.

Chapter 16

Opening Up Real Insurance Competition

Along similar lines, the other area of improvement that states can make is, open up the door and approve more insurance policies to increase competition among insurers. The more insurers can compete within a state, the better the pricing will become. It goes right back to mathematical economics; the more companies that sell similar products, the cheaper the consumer prices of that product or service will become, this helps to attract consumers to a particular brand, because for consumers, price matters.

Insurance departments can impact the overall cost of health insurance by loosening restrictions and incentivizing insurance companies to create new health policies that would meet market demands. As an example, when a person looses their job instead of just two options of COBRA or purchasing individual coverage options; insurance departments could encourage insurers to provide a modified health policy that featured significantly reduced premiums. They could even provide what other insurances provide, which is called a continuation of coverage provision that continues coverage without a premium for a specified period of time.

As a matter of fact, state departments of insurance are more than capable of working together with insurers to come up with insurance solutions that meet the demands of the population of their respective states. We certainly don't need a Washington Bureaucracy to make decisions on what works for every person in every state, what works in Connecticut won't work in Florida and vice versa. After all, they live in Washington full time, so how would they know what the people of Tahlequah Oklahoma health insurance needs are? Go ahead and try to pronounce it, it is a real place.

Here's a specific way the state insurance departments can help where The DocNet solution is implemented; they can request from insurers, submissions of major medical plans that would separate the health services component that we've described, then they would expedite the approval of those plans for sale in their respective state. Simple enough!

Now competition is something that even the Obama administration believes in, I say that because they promote the idea of competition in the insurance exchanges as new means by which insurers must compete, which according to them will help lower rates. Healthcare.gov defines the exchanges as:

A new transparent and competitive insurance marketplace where individuals and small businesses can buy affordable and qualified health benefit plans. Affordable Insurance Exchanges will offer you a choice of health plans that meet certain benefits and cost standards.

Given that, it would seem that competition is a critical aspect to the necessary cost cutting measures which will need to be enacted in order to help achieve affordable insurance. Each state needs to attract more insurance companies, by making it easier for them to be approved to do business. And they need to approve new and innovative policies to assist consumers in reducing their premiums.

We simply believe that the free market can handle creating the competition and innovation required to overcome this challenge, without government intervention and a trillion dollar price tag charged to the national credit card.

Chapter 17

The Remedy to Uncompensated Care

As we discussed before, uncompensated care amounts to billions of dollars that hospitals are forced to absorb, and it's costing all of us. But the problem is how can we turn our backs on those who need medical help and then call ourselves humane. We simply can't.

Given that we can't, we must find alternative solutions to this escalating problem. There is a three part answer to this problem and the first we've already discussed, and that is charity and faith based funding, to help those who, otherwise, would be left to fend for themselves, so we won't revisit that solution, but to emphasize the importance and opportunity for these groups to make a difference.

The second solution to this problem is to revisit the history of the first hospital in America. Benjamin Franklin went to the Philadelphia Assembly and got them to agree to match funds to create a hospital for the purpose of helping the sick and insane in Philadelphia.

We too, must come up with local solutions to meet the demands of our communities for the betterment of that community. It could be in the creation of public health clinics funded by research grants. For our more liberal leaning Americans, voters could even make it a ballot measure to pay for these centers through taxes if they choose to, every area could decide for itself. It could be a public and private cooperation or any number of other possibilities that the local community can, through the knowledge of what their community needs, create the approach to tackle this problem.

The last point is that we must address the illegal immigrant impact on our social services and in particularly our public health costs as it relates to uncompensated care. We pointed out before that 25% of all uncompensated care derived from the illegal immigrant population in America. If you support illegal immigration, that's fine, but those who are for it, find a way to fund the expense of it, because, as a matter of pure mathematics, we can't afford the costs any longer.

And listen before you start throwing around the "you're a racist" manipulation, allow me to say that I don't blame one single illegal immigrant for coming here to find work or to better their situation, but, I do blame our own government for not making it easier for those who want to come here, to come through the front door. My brother-in-law spend over 20 years of his life trying to move his family to America from the Philippines and the cost, plus the time it takes to get approvals for multiple people, prevented him from ever achieving that dream, and he died having never set foot on American soil.

So, I am all for legal immigration. I support making it much easier for those who want to be Americans to come here and assimilate into the American way of life. But, if we're honest about what's happening here, we've allowed corporations and politicians to enslave people by giving them false hope of citizenship. It doesn't take a genius to understand that no one who supports illegal immigration really cares for these folks, the political parties or the citizens that use illegal immigrant workers don't have any intentions of helping them achieve that goal. So, truthfully, if you support illegal immigration then you support modernized slavery, and that's unfortunate.

What's sad is, that I have to include this explanation in anticipation of the outcry of racism as a sort of legal disclaimer or something, just because I'm trying to point out the cause and effect of an issue. Regardless, I'm going to say what needs to be said, and if to you think I'm a racist, then so be it!

As it relates to health costs, the illegal immigrant population is a factor, and we desperately need a solution; if the nation does nothing to stop the flow of illegal immigrants, then we must insist that the groups who support and encourage illegal immigration, like LULAC, LARASA as well as so many other including churches. Then they should take the responsibility to set up healthcare funds to pay the costs and stop passing it on to everyone else.

Look, if I go to Mexico, El Salvador or any Central or South American country, I would never be afforded healthcare without the ability to pay for it. Americans shouldn't have to carry the burden of the world on our shoulders except through the personal choice of charity. Simply, if you support the illegal immigration in any way, then pay for it! That's all we're asking for as the paying consumers of healthcare and taxpayers of America.

Chapter 18

The Conclusion

So in conclusion, let me just point out, that many parts of this plan are very similar to others ideas about how to resolve our health cost woes; and with some effort, those provisions can be readily implemented. Many might believe that The DocNet is a solution that would take an overwhelming amount of time to begin to realize its benefits, but I would flatly disagree.

Doctors and patients could begin the process immediately, and quite frankly, no one could stop them from doing so, at least not if you live in a business friendly state, because it's a transaction between a consumer and a business.

The advantage of a doctor taking the lead and making The DocNet available to patients is, it has an immediate impact on the problem. By covering the patient's care and not making a claim with an insurer, we start to reduce the overall costs of the smaller claims and the administrative costs associated to them.

When enough patients are being cared for under The DocNet, and the claims experience begins to shift in a positive direction, insurance companies and government entities will have no choice but to acknowledge its success. That's when we'll have reached the tipping point, and see the downhill slide toward a complete implementation of this free market solution.

The best part is that we don't have to wait for the politicians to come to any kind of consensus on the issue or debate the overall costs. If charities and doctors would begin now to treat the poor without compensation from the patients, or file claims with government agencies, then we could realize quite quickly a reduction in the health costs to our states, leaving more monies in the general fund for other needs like fixing the roads or reduce our taxes.

If the federal government could ever reach an agreement, to move from a fee for service payment structure, to a premium support model, we realize a $400 plus billion savings immediately.

The bottom line, we solve this problem through the innovations of entrepreneurialism and government scarcity. By lowering the costs of coverage and health services, you'll attract more consumers into the market. When they are covered, they are no longer a drag on the paying healthcare public or taxpayers, that helps reduces the costs for the government programs, and doesn't leave hospitals and government to pick up the tab, when they don't pay their bill. That helps us all.

I admit, I am one guy who's only sold health and supplemental insurances for the last twenty years, but I hold no loyalties to any insurance company, because my loyalty has always been to my clients. What I've witnessed over just the last ten years of my career is a system becoming massively complicated, and worse, ineffective in solving the healthcare needs of the consumers of whom they are supposed to be serving.

It's time for a change in strategy, and I believe that the solutions that I've presented here, are a good course to set, to secure the free market healthcare industry for the foreseeable future. And to those who would criticize this plan, before you do, tell me, what's your plan?

I want to say thank you to all of you who took the time and allowed me to share this idea with you, and I pray it'll catch on, and help bring us closer to a real solution to this continual problem.

As I've said many times throughout this book, we are Americans, and we don't settle for anyone messing with us or our freedoms…. do we?

If we do, then all I can say is that the America I know, the one I was willing to defend has finally succumbed to her wounds of progressive tyranny, and patriots are needed to revive her. But I refuse to believe that this is the end of America and her exceptionalism. We've never backed down from a fight, and we shouldn't start now. The socialization of our healthcare system is a leap in the wrong direction, but we've been on the brink before throughout our history, and when we're reminded of what freedoms we'll lose, Americans take a stand to fight for that freedom. That's who we really are.

I will admit that we are at a critical juncture in our history, and it must be taken seriously. We need to stand on what God and the founders of our nation created, and address our grievances with this government and demand that this dangerous healthcare bill, be repealed and that the government get out of the business of taking care of people, and worry about protecting us from those who seek to destroy us and nothing more.

The time is now for bold ideas, and I'm calling on every American, to step up and be willing to push for bold ideas driven by what has always made us great -- the free market. If you have an idea, send it to me and together we can present ideas that can solve the problems of today without the need for more government solutions.

To all my fellow Veterans I say God Bless you for your service, your country owes you a debt deeper than just of gratitude. And to all my fellow Americans I say may God Bless each of you and God Bless the United States of America!

###

Now that you've read how we could solve the health costs crisis in America, would you do me the honor of leaving your thoughts about it at one of your favorite book retailers?

I've provided links to two of the most popular below.

http://amzn.com/B007OLH2UE

http://www.barnesandnoble.com/w/the-docnet-keven-card/1111560473?ean=2940014491402

About the Author

Keven is a common sense, straightforward and compassionate motivational speaker and life trainer. He utilizes his own life experiences and personal faith to help others to face and conquer their challenges and to regain their power as they learn to see life from a fresh perspective.

He is a passionate and committed man which is reflected both in his strong relationship with God and the love of his life, his wife, Marianne. He is a devoted father to his four wonderful children, Stephanie, Branden, Izabella and the newest addition, baby Kaela.

He has been a life and health insurance agent for nearly 20 years. It's through that experience he has a unique perspective of what the challenges are with the health cost crisis of America. As an entrepreneur he also understands the values of the free market. The combination of that experience gives Keven the expertise to design a comprehensive free market alternative demonstrated in The DocNet.

Also as a former U.S. Marine he has demonstrated his willingness to fight for freedom and to defend the Constitution of the United States. He believes strongly that freedom itself is at risk under the misguided legislation we termed Obamacare.

If you love your country and want to see freedom restored then you have something in common with Keven. Together you can make a stand for the freedom that America has always known and enjoyed by standing for a free market solution and then sharing that solution with other freedom loving Americans.

May God Continue to Bless America!

Other literary work on Amazon: <u>Forever Newlyweds</u>

Connect With Me Online:

Facebook: <u>http://facebook.com/thechristianrepublic</u>

Twitter: <u>http://twitter.com/thechristianrep</u>

OR

Facebook: <u>http://facebook.com/kevencard</u>

Twitter: <u>http://twitter.com/kevencard</u>

My Blogs: <u>http://thechristianrepublic.com</u> or
<u>http://kevencard.com</u>

Bibliography (Not in particular order):

Creation of the First Hospital: Pennsylvania Hospital
http://www.uphs.upenn.edu/paharc/features/creation.html

Senator Ben Nelson
http://bennelson.senate.gov/%20/t%20_blank

Senator Mary Landrieu
http://landrieu.senate.gov/%20/t%20_blank

Senator Jim Webb gives up re-election bid over healthcare
reform:
http://www.politico.com/blogs/bensmith/0211/Source_Webb_won
t_seek_reelection.html

The Breakdown of Obamacare by The Heritage Foundation:
http://www.heritage.org/research/reports/2011/01/obamacare-
and-the-individual-mandate-violating-personal-liberty-and-
federalism

Total population from Census Bureau:
http://www.census.gov/main/www/popclock.html

CBO nearly doubles estimated costs of Obamacare:
http://www.foxnews.com/politics/2012/03/14/cbo-health-law-
estimate-shows-much-higher-spending-beyond-first-10-years/

What is a Supermajority?
http://en.wikipedia.org/wiki/Supermajority

Number of uninsured in America according to Fact Check:
http://www.factcheck.org/2009/09/thirty-million-uninsured/

6 Pages of Obamacare Equals 429 Pages of Regulations:
http://www.usnews.com/news/washington-
whispers/articles/2011/04/07/6-pages-of-obamacare-equals-429-
pages-of-regulations

The Fight Over Contraception Mandate - The Hill:
http://thehill.com/blogs/healthwatch/abortion/191307-gop-dems-
battle-over-health-laws-contraceptive-coverage

Announcement that the Obama Administration would not compromise any further on Contraception Mandate: http://www.nytimes.com/2012/03/17/health/policy/obama-administration-says-birth-control-mandate-applies-to-religious-groups-that-insure-themselves.html

Clinton 1999 State of Union Address to Target Tobacco Companies: http://www.washingtonpost.com/wp-srv/politics/special/clinton/stories/president012099.htm

Children's Health Insurance Program of 2009: http://en.wikipedia.org/wiki/Children%27s_Health_Insurance_Program_Reauthorization_Act_of_2009%20/o%20Children's%20Health%20Insurance%20Program%20Reauthorization%20Act%20of%202009

Obama Administration to cut Veteran Health Benefits: http://freebeacon.com/trashing-tricare/

Blue Cross Blue Shield Report on health cost breakdown - 87% goes out in claims and claims costs: http://www.bcbstx.com/pdf/eco_health_care_1_brochure_tx.pdf

Decline of Competition in New York: http://www.27east.com/news/article.cfm/East-End/404493/Source-Empire-Blue-Cross-Blue-Shield-Set-To-Drop-Most-Of-Its-Small-Group-Plans-In-New-York

Cigna to drop small group health plans: http://blogs.courant.com/connecticut_insurance/2010/10/cigna-wont-offer-smallgroup-pl.html

USA Today reports on the coming doctor shortage: http://www.usatoday.com/news/health/2009-08-17-doctor-gp-shortage_N.htm

Association of American Medical Colleges calls for lift on
Medicare funded residencies:
https://www.aamc.org/newsroom/reporter/april11/184178/addres
sing_the_physician_shortage_under_reform.html

Georgia Health Sciences University talks about income disparity:
http://medicalpartnership.usg.edu/research/collaborations/addres
sing_the_physician_shortage

The costs of frivolous lawsuits:
http://blogs.wsj.com/numbersguy/how-much-are-frivolous-
lawsuits-really-costing-you-95/

Study of how many doctors practice defensive medicine:
http://www.aaos.org/news/aaosnow/dec10/advocacy2.asp

Texas Insurance Mandates:
http://www.tdi.texas.gov/hmo/documents/lhmanben.pdf

Obama criticizes insurance companies:
http://www.csmonitor.com/USA/Politics/2010/0308/To-advance-
healthcare-reform-Obama-comes-down-on-insurers

Washington Post's Sarah Kliff says doctors in America are paid
too much: http://www.washingtonpost.com/blogs/ezra-
klein/post/should-the-doc-fix-get-
fixed/2011/12/20/gIQAkxr76O_blog.html

Doctors are giving up their Medicare patients:
http://www.usatoday.com/news/washington/2010-06-20-
medicare_N.htm

The cost of hospital closures as a result of uncompensated care:
http://archive.newsmax.com/archives/articles/2005/12/26/170334
.shtml

Cost of illegal immigration uncompensated care on healthcare:
http://www.jpands.org/vol10no1/cosman.pdf

Wall Street Journal report of future doctor shortage:
http://online.wsj.com/article/SB10001424052702304506904575180331528424238.html

Average Family Doctor Patient load is 2148:
http://www.primcare.vcu.edu/manpower/sld004.htm

AMA Calculation for optimum patient Load: 2392:
http://www.ama-assn.org/amednews/2008/05/12/bisa0512.htm

What is a physicians Assistant:
http://physicianassistantcareer.com/

Average Labs per disease
http://ajcp.ascpjournals.org/content/116/6/879.full.pdf

Costs per Lab work
http://www.yourhealthlab.com/tests.asp

Insurance Premium Dollar Breakdown
http://www.bcbstx.com/pdf/eco_health_care_1_brochure_tx.pdf

Healthcare cost breakdown National Institute for Healthcare
Management
http://www.changehealthcare.com/downloads/industry/2011.07%
20NIHCM-CostBrief.pdf

Medicare pays 25% less than private Insurance
http://www.washingtonpost.com/wp-
dyn/content/article/2010/06/18/AR2010061804700.html

How Much Doctors Make (Supply and Demand)
http://www.forbes.com/2010/02/11/how-much-does-a-doctor-
make-business-healthcare-doctors.html

https://www.aamc.org/students/considering/exploring_medical/

Lawsuit for underpayments to doctors from Medicare
http://www.ama-assn.org/amednews/2011/03/14/gvsb0314.htm

Refusal of Congress to let Americans buy medicine from Canada
http://articles.orlandosentinel.com/2010-05-02/news/os-drugs-
canada-online-20100502_1_doughnut-hole-canadian-online-
pharmacy-drugs

How much do lawsuits cost medical industry?
http://www.triallawyersinc.com/healthcare/hc01.html
http://www.heartland.org/policybot/results/18270/Litigation_Raisi
ng_Health_Care_Costs_Study_Says.html

Cost of Defensive Medicine:
http://www.aaos.org/news/aaosnow/nov08/managing7.asp
http://online.wsj.com/article/SB125193312967181349.html
http://blogs.wsj.com/health/2010/09/07/how-much-does-defensive-medicine-cost-one-study-says-46-billion/

Medical Malpractice Insurance:
http://online.wsj.com/article/SB125193312967181349.html

Affects of Tort Reform:
http://www.cbo.gov/doc.cfm?index=5549&type=0&sequence=1
http://www.tortreform.com/node/926
http://blogs.wsj.com/health/2008/05/19/doctors-flock-to-texas-after-tort-reform/

Healthcare.gov defines competition
http://www.healthcare.gov/glossary/e/exchange.html

CNN Money: The number of people on government healthcare rises:
http://money.cnn.com/2011/09/13/news/economy/census_bureau_health_insurance/

CMS calculations for US spending on Healthcare:
https://www.cms.gov/NationalHealthExpendData/02_NationalHealthAccountsHistorical.asp

An Act For the Relief of Sick and Disabled Seaman…created by 5th Congress:
http://www.scribd.com/doc/29099806/Act-for-the-Relief-of-Sick-DisabledSeamen-July-1798

Essex Hospital (Story during Revolutionary period):
http://en.wikipedia.org/wiki/Essex_hospital
http://www.npr.org/templates/story/story.php?storyId=113543985

Provision in Obamacare force Catholic Hospital to pay for birth control:
http://www.theblaze.com/stories/religious-organizations-object-to-new-government-birth-control-requirements/

America Loosing medical inventions edge to China:
http://www.11alive.com/news/article/187674/40/US-Losing-Edge-in-Medical-Inventions-and-Innovation

Obama's Medicare Plan: Rationing by Bureaucrats:
http://www.weeklystandard.com/blogs/obamas-bureaucratic-vision-medicare-spending_557412.html

WSJ: Doctor shortage 150,000 in 15 years:
http://online.wsj.com/article/SB10001424052702304506904575180331528424238.html

CVS Monetary breakdown:
http://blogs.wpri.com/2011/02/22/cvs-by-the-numbers-1-2-billion-prescriptions/

75% of drugs have generic equivalent:
http://www.usatoday.com/news/washington/judicial/supremecourtopinions/2011-06-23-supreme-court-drug-warning-label_n.htm

Cost compare of generic and brand name drugs:
http://www.bcbsm.com/pdf/ps_generic.pdf

Generics outgrowing estimates:
http://www.gao.gov/new.items/d11306r.pdf

http://www.dailyfinance.com/2011/03/16/prescription-drug-prices-still-growing-strong/

http://www.foxbusiness.com/personal-finance/2011/03/16/prescription-drug-prices-growing-strong/

Medical Loss Ratio:
http://www.buckconsultants.com/buckconsultants/portals/0/documents/PUBLICATIONS/Newsletters/FYI/2011/FYI-01-24-11-HHS-Issues-Medical-Loss-Ratio-and-Rate-Increase-Review-Regulations.pdf

Medicare Actuaries say: Obamacare would cause 14 Million to lose health insurance:
http://www.foxnews.com/politics/2010/04/22/health-care-law-increase-costs-experts-conclude-new-report/

Clinton announces he'll sue tobacco companies for medical costs:
http://www.washingtonpost.com/wp-srv/politics/special/clinton/stories/president012099.htm

Illegal Immigration "permanent patients" driving up hospital costs:
http://www.theblaze.com/stories/hospitals-stuck-with-illegal-immigrant-uninsured-permanent-patients-at-massive-cost/

CDC (48.1% of medical care received in primary care physician office):
http://www.cdc.gov/nchs/data/series/sr_13/sr13_169.pdf

Obama Administration Mandates contraception coverage over Catholic Protests:
http://www.theblaze.com/stories/obama-admin-mandates-religious-employers-cover-contraception-cost-catholic-bishops-furious/

Primary Care Doctor Shortage:
http://journals.gmu.edu/index.php/newvoices/article/viewFile/258/159

http://www.usatoday.com/news/health/2009-08-17-doctor-gp-shortage_N.htm

The arm distance Doctor Patient relationship:
http://www.nytimes.com/2011/04/23/health/23doctor.html?pagewanted=all

Texas solution to frivolous lawsuits:
http://www.bobdorigojones.com/2011/01/15/a-texas-sized-bold-idea-for-eliminating-frivolous-lawsuits/

American Academy of Orthopedic Surgeons breakdown of defensive medicine:
http://www.aaos.org/news/aaosnow/dec10/advocacy2.asp

Texas Department of Insurance mandates:
http://www.tdi.texas.gov/hmo/documents/lhmanben.pdf

Uncompensated Care:
http://www.aha.org/research/rc/stat-studies/Studies.shtml

Illegal Aliens and American Medicine:
http://www.jpands.org/vol10no1/cosman.pdf

Hospital closures due to uncompensated care:
http://archive.newsmax.com/archives/articles/2005/12/26/170334.shtml

2010 Census Data Report:
http://www.census.gov/prod/2011pubs/p60-239.pdf

US Healthcare Dollars Where it came from and where it went from CMS.gov:
https://www.cms.gov/NationalHealthExpendData/downloads/PieChartSourcesExpenditures2010.pdf

The amount of state contributions to Medicaid as based on Texas: (page 16):
http://www.hhsc.state.tx.us/hb-497_122010.pdf

US Federal Expenditure Breakdown:
http://www.usgovernmentspending.com/year_spending_2011USbt_13bs1s_1017

Association of American Medical Colleges:
https://www.aamc.org/newsroom/reporter/april11/184178/addressing_the_physician_shortage_under_reform.html

Income Disparity of Doctors from Georgia Health Sciences University:
http://medicalpartnership.usg.edu/research/collaborations/addressing_the_physician_shortage

Texas Tort Reform
http://www.tortreform.com/node/926

http://www.aaos.org/news/aaosnow/dec10/advocacy2.asp

Wall Street Journal Report on benefits of Texas tort reform:
http://blogs.wsj.com/health/2008/05/19/doctors-flock-to-texas-after-tort-reform/

Apple sets up shop in Texas:
http://www.reuters.com/article/2011/12/16/us-apple-samsung-idUSTRE7BF0D420111216

GOP alternative to Obamacare:
http://www.gop.gov/indepth/pledge/healthcare

Heritage on Obamacare:
http://www.heritage.org/initiatives/health-care

Heritage Medicare Reform:
http://www.heritage.org/research/reports/2012/02/premium-support-is-incremental-not-radical-medicare-reform

New CBO $1.76 Trillion estimate on Obamacare:
http://www.foxnews.com/politics/2012/03/14/cbo-health-law-estimate-shows-much-higher-spending-beyond-first-10-years/

Business cost increase due to compliance with Obamacare:
http://www.workforce.com/article/20120309/NEWS01/120309955/survey-health-care-reform-law-driving-employers-group-health-costs-up

Kathleen Sebelius on using Obamacare to fund abortion:
http://youtu.be/uCmFFDyDrv8

Obama on 15 year transition of employer based system:
http://youtu.be/wtbfPOgKf2g

Candidate Obama states clearly that he wants a single payer system: http://youtu.be/V0ER4rhpwlM

American Academy of Orthopedic Surgeons study of defensive medicine:
http://www.aaos.org/news/aaosnow/dec10/advocacy2.asp

Obama Administration clarifies position on contraception mandate (NY Times):
http://www.nytimes.com/2012/03/17/health/policy/obama-administration-says-birth-control-mandate-applies-to-religious-groups-that-insure-themselves.html

www.ingramcontent.com/pod-product-compliance
Lightning Source LLC
Chambersburg PA
CBHW022247290526
45785CB00015B/377